A QUICK TING ON...
...ABOUT THE SERIES

A Quick Ting On is an idea rooted in archiving all things Black British culture. It is a book series dedicated to Black Britishness and all the ways this identity expands and grows. Each book in the series focuses on a singular topic that is of cultural importance to Black Britishness (and beyond), giving it the sole focus it deserves. The series was inspired by everyday conversations had with Black British folk far and wide, whether that be in WhatsApp group chats, in person, on social media, at parties, barbecues and so on.

A Quick Ting On is about providing an arena for Black people to archive things that they deem important to them and in turn allowing these explorations to exist long after we are here.

A bundle of joy, learning, nostalgia and home.

Magdalene Abraha FRSA (Mags)
xx

PRAISE FOR A QUICK TING ON...

'Groundbreaking,' *The Guardian*

'Amazing,' *The Metro*

'Timely and needed,' BBC Radio 5

'Spearheaded by the hugely impressive Magdalene Abraha, the heartening launch of a phenomenal new series,' Mellville House

'There is nothing like this,' *The Bookseller*

'What better way to begin Black History Month than with the announcement of a book series celebrating Black British life?' *Bustle* Magazine

'Magdalene Abraha will launch her long-awaited book series, *A Quick Ting On…* it's brilliant,' *Elle*

'Exciting,' *Refinery29*

'The first ever non-fiction book of its kind', *The Voice*

'*A Quick Ting On…* is set to be behind some of the most exciting books.' *Stylist* Magazine

'A game changer,' BBC World Service

'Bringing Black Britishness to the fore,' *The Blacklist*

'How much do you know about plantains? Or Black British Businesses? Or Afrobeats? If your answer is not enough, that could soon be rectified,' *Evening Standard*

A QUICK TING ON...

PLANTAIN

RUI DA SILVA

AQ
TO

JACARANDA

This edition first published in Great Britain 2022
Jacaranda Books Art Music Ltd
27 Old Gloucester Street,
London WC1N 3AX
www.jacarandabooksartmusic.co.uk

A CIP catalogue record for this book is available from the British
Library

ISBN: 9781913090531
eISBN: 9781913090562

Cover Illustration: Camilla Ru
Cover Design: Baker, bplanb.co.uk
Typeset by: Kamillah Brandes

TO MY DEAREST AND TRUEST
FRIENDS:

PLEASE STOP INVITING ME TO PLACES
THAT DON'T SERVE PLANTAIN.

I'M TIRED.

CONTENTS

PREFACE

And with that. Hi and let me welcome you to the world's first, most dedicated love letter to one of Mother Nature's greatest gifts. In fact, this entire work framed as a book for you is in reality one long consolidated page of my diary. A testament to the fruit that has kept me going all these years. Manifested in 100+ pages of Plantain-powered word vomit. Still, I invite you to stick around. Because if you like Plantain, love Plantain, don't know Plantain, never heard of Plantain and all the above, this book is for you. And even if you don't like Plantain (red flag). Give this book a try and I promise you'll have a newfound appreciation for the world's greatest fruit. Yes, I claim it.

In this book, if that's what we're calling it, we won't be holding an inquiry or debate about how great Plantain is. That's an undeniable truth. Plantain's value as a culinary treasure is verified. Bluetick status and all. Instead, this book focuses on the story of Plantain that we rarely get the chance to hear. The 'Whys', 'Hows' and 'Whos' that make the fruit what it is.

This book is the story of Plantain, written by a true and dear Plantain-lover.

So boom. Wag1. My name is Rui. Rui Da Silva. No, not the white Portuguese DJ that appears when you search my name on Google. Rui Da Silva, the third of his name, named after my father, named after his father. I was born in Portugal. My parents brought me to Babylon, England, when I was three. We moved into a small estate in North London and I have been galavanting in and around the city ever since.

From the moment I could walk, I have been testing the limits of my decision-making. It started with scraping my bare knees on floors, leaving storytelling scars. It soon turned into jumping off roofs. Flying off of swings, landing face first. Graffiting on school walls. Playing 5 Alive*, run-outs** and knock down-ginger*** way past my curfew. Searching far and wide for the steepest and scariest hill to ride my only pedal bike down. Breaking bones. Breaking locks. Breaking laws. Securing whines****. Running from the police. Sleeping outside. Travelling across borders with no money. Performing on stages with a broken laptop and the list goes on.

The things I've done in my life have been, in one way or another, in search of one thing—happiness. We all have this in

---

* A game that takes place with two or more people. Involving a football and a wall. The players kick the ball against the wall, each at a time only allowing the ball to bounce once on the ground before they can kick it. If a player lets the ball bounce on the floor more than once before they kick it, they lose a life. Each player has five lives, with the first person to get to zero losing the game.

** A game that takes place with five or more players. One person plays as 'It' or the 'guard', standing next to a lamppost or something similar and this is called the 'home base'. The rest of the group 'runs out' and hide while the guard counts to 40, 50 or 60. The guard then has to find everyone and touch them before they can get back to home base and say 'safe'. Anyone who's touched by the guard is out. The players can't speak to each other but they can help distract the guard.

*** The name of a children's street game dating from the early 19th century where children knock on doors and then run away before the door is answered.

**** Known as Caribbean slang. Securing a whine is when one person successfully initiates a dance with another. Usually in a party or in an environment where bashment, reggae or music of similar rhythm and tempo is playing. This usually involves little to no verbal communication. Instead, relying on body language, eye contact and subtle cues.

common. Our eternal search for the 'ahh life is good' moment. We work hard for it and when we finally get it, it leaves as fast as it came. It slips through our fingers and we look for the cheapest or most expensive way to get it back. The best moments, though, are the ones you know you can get back. The ones you can rely on tomorrow as you did today. As you're reading this you're likely trying to think about what your thing is. As you think, let me tell you mine. If it isn't already obvious.

Drum roll, please.

PLANTAIN!

For me, Plantain is the gift that keeps on giving. There is dizzy joy in every bite that leaves me coming back for more. Plantain to me (and many like me) is one of the most underrated modern-day cultural artefacts of the world. A boastful claim I know. But beyond its delectable culinary appeal, Plantain also has a wider social value. Its value as a source of global sustenance, celebration and other things, scores much higher than its price tag. In many ways, the fruit is also like a dot. A cultural indicator if you'd like. Connecting transatlantic histories of Afro-Caribbean people in the heart of Babylon. To explain. Food, like art, like music, can tell us stories about the communities they come from. When we look at how communities consume their food, how do they create it, and why, we uncover deeper stories about who these communities are, their histories, so on and so forth. Plantain is no different. Using Plantain, you can trace stories of communities in almost every crevice of the world, highlighting its diversity and its resourcefulness, globally. So when I say Plantain is the 13th Wonder of the World, you may laugh, but by the time you are through with this book, you too will understand the magical beauty that is Plantain.

Before I go into the Plantain of it all, let me start by telling you how this book even came about.

So, some years ago, for my 22nd or 23rd birthday, a good friend of mine decided to treat me to a surprise birthday dinner and with that, a promise of a gift. A gift, I should add, that she was confident I would love. At this point, alarm bells started ringing.

Generally speaking, I don't expect birthday gifts from anyone outside the family. For one, my birthday is on the 22nd December. Amidst Christmas shopping hype and with Boxing Day and New Year's in the same period, everyone's funds are low or going elsewhere. Adding to that, receiving presents is a risky game. There's always a possibility that I'll be looking at what's in my hands and wondering, 'why?', wearing a counterfeit smile to boot. Don't worry, if you're reading this, I absolutely loved what you got me.

So the closer to the time, my curiosity for what she had gotten had grown. What was it? Why was she so sure I would like it? How should I prep my counterfeit smile?

We met up at a fancy-ish location. Somewhere off Shoreditch High Street station. So not that fancy. We walked past whatever the contemporary word for hipsters is. The whole time I suppressed my curiosity to ask what she had gotten me. I stayed patient.

When we reached the restaurant, the lights inside were dim. The decor was reminiscent of what I imagine a Southeast Asian museum would look like. We were both donning full tracksuits. My friend was in Adidas while I was in a Nike ting and if I remember correctly we also arrived a little late. A little late meaning the kitchen was closing and hardly any other customers were around. Quite typical for both of us.

We sat down and ordered, but I wasn't eating much. My friend asked me whether I liked the food, knowing I eat twice as much as her.

The food was alright but something was eating at me instead. The curiosity for what my birthday gift might have been finally reached its peak.

As I was readying to thank her for the dinner, she reached into her bag and with a sly smile revealed what she had gotten me. What I had been waiting for the whole time.

From her bag, she pulled what looked like wrapped, bendy ornaments. For the first second or so I was confused. But as soon as I saw the full shape of the gift wrapping, I knew exactly what it was. The day was never to be forgotten. It was a gift that holds a special place in our friendship and the reason you're reading this book.

To get straight to the point, for my 22nd, or 23rd birthday, my good good friend bought me Plantain. Gift-wrapped.

And that's where this book starts. Over the years. My pronounced fondness for Plantain has far outweighed my enthusiasm for anything else. Have you ever seen the video of the kid who gets an avocado for Christmas and beams? Search 'Boy gets Avocado for Christmas' on YouTube, the video is currently at over 1.2million views. That is me but with Plantain.

I don't know why my zeal for Plantain is as strong as it is. It conquers my usual tendency to be reserved or ambivalent about any and everything else. I claim my love of Plantain with all my chest and clarity of speech. Chances are if you've got to know me well over the years, you've heard me comment on how wonderful Plantain is. For me, there's a quality of certainty when it comes to Plantain that cannot be shaken. It cannot be questioned and it cannot be corrupted. You know how grass is green. The sky is blue and roses are red. Well, in that same vein, Plantain is Plantain. Which is to say, Plantain is the best!

My love for Plantain was the catalyst for my friend getting me the fruit as my birthday gift. It was also what led to this book. To explain, this same friend of mine is a publisher. A brilliant one at that. One day she sent me a WhatsApp message saying, 'would you like to write a book on Plantain?'. The thought of it made me laugh and I responded by entertaining the idea as if it were a joke. Until I realised she was being dead serious. Next thing you know, I am looking at editorial deadlines and word counts. She might have banged juj*.

As it goes, she introduced me to her idea for her *A Quick Ting On* series and more importantly *A Quick Ting On: Plantain*. Now, here we are.

So thank you, Maggy, my good sis and publisher for making this happen. She's great. And if you end up enjoying what I have to say in this book, you can thank Magdalene. You can thank your delivery driver who brought you the parcel. The cashier of the book store if we aren't in lockdown by the time you read this. But really and truly, we all ought to thank the greater good that made this all possible. The positive and motivating force within my life—Plantain. Thank you for being you.

There are many variations of the fruit's name. Plæntem for my West Africans (because God gave us wisdom). Plæntm if you're Caribbean, Plátano for our Latin American brethren and there are more.

Being part of the Black diaspora, I'll be exploring Plantain from a Black British lens. Referring to the experiences of African and Caribbean Brits alike, both large and influential

---

*   Derived mainly from cultures across West Africa. Juj or Juju refers to a practice of magic used by people with spellbinding abilities. Originally, a cult practice by witches, witch doctors and unorthodox priests. Juju has now developed into a much less bizarre cultural reference. Powered by myths, unexplained events, folklore and rumours. Juju is heavily referenced across the Black diaspora for events that don't seem to have a rational explanation.

communities in the UK. Many of which have the fruit, sacred in the heart of their kitchens. To capture the depth of the Black British Plantain culture is no easy task but I'll try init.

So now, back to the restaurant. After singing her praises and taking several pictures with my new trophy gift, I placed the Plantains in my bag. Then upon arriving home that night, I stashed them in my kitchen. The following week I fried them in baths of virgin olive oil. The week-long wait meant its skin had matured at a perfect but modest sweetness.

I sliced the fruit with precision into what can be described as slanted cylinder oval shapes. I sprinkled a bit of salt, then slipped them into a frying pan with extreme dexterity. There I watched as they sizzled into beautiful golden brown pieces. Once cooked to my liking, I removed them from the oil with care. I placed them on two stacked sheets of tissue to soak up the oil. Then for the finale. I pierced each piece with a lucky fork and ate them with grace, achieving complete culinary satisfaction.

This is a process I repeat and have been repeating almost every other week for the majority of my life.

Now before this turns into an extended personal account of how many ways I can say, 'I love Plantain', I'd like to say that this book isn't a personal memoir. Though at times it might read like one. A marvel of Plantain is the tens, if not, hundreds of millions of people around the world who share the love for it. People who have come to know and appreciate Plantain in the same ways I have and even more so. From growers and exporters, importers and chefs to the average consumers.

In my earlier years, I thought Plantain was something that only took place in my family home. I grew up in a majority white community and didn't know any better. It wasn't until I started sourcing it myself that I realised the many communities that also indulged.

Being from São Tomé (a central African island). Born in Portugal. Raised in England, having attended a majority white primary and secondary school. The things that helped me embrace my cultural background were of huge importance, especially outside of my home environment. Whether it was music, language, clothing or food. Even in the early days of African culture becoming more popular in school, I still felt a bit alienated. African culture seems like something everyone's privy to now but back then, it was far from cool. It was in my late secondary school years when things began to shift ever so slightly and we entered a new era. This era would house the early stages of West African identity becoming attractive. From being F.O.B* to being everyone's favourite comedian. Today, youth culture seems to fundamentally include African culture and ideals. African identity in the scope of Black Britain has come a long way.

Still. When this cultural shift began, it didn't entirely reflect PALOP culture. What is a PALOP you ask? A PALOP is an African country where Portuguese is the national language. There are six of us. São Tomé (where my family are from). Mozambique. Angola. Cape Verde. Guinea-Bissau and Equatorial Guinea. For us, our cultures didn't as easily surface with the bits of West African culture becoming more popular. (Because African identity is not a monolith).

Our parents didn't exactly sound like the renditions of West African vernacular shared in new waves of slang. We couldn't

---

*   'Fresh Off the Boat' is a slur used towards immigrant communities. Particularly African diasporas.

care less about the Jollof wars. And it would be a while before we heard Kuduro or Kizomba in the Afrobeat segments of the rave. That is not to say there aren't many similarities and shared experiences. In fact, one thing that we seemed to all relate to was the love of Plantain.

Plantain, I found, was appreciated the same way in my culture as it was across other Black communities. Plantain in this sense was a culinary equalizer. Bringing together a large part of the Black diaspora. Seen on social media, where the Black-Twitter-Plantain-Loving-Crew reign strong. A scour through Twitter reveals hundreds, if not thousands of 'Plantain appreciation tweets'. Despite our disagreements on ideal ripeness and correct pronunciation. Our passion for Plantain unites us. In a unanimous understanding of its importance and its fantabulousness.

One of my most favourite ever Plantain tweets is one user's assertion that:

'Smoking breaks at work should be deducted from annual leave. We all have addictions, you don't see me leave a meeting to fry Plantain.'

This appreciation extends beyond the borders of the Black Community. An enjoyable part of writing this book was learning about the other cultures where Plantain also shines. From the Philippines, where there are many versions of Plantain. To the Dominican Republic, where unripe Plantain can be used to make 'Mangu'. Plantain boiled in saltwater then mashed with margarine or butter. Or in India, where the Malayali people have 'Sadyha'. A feast of vegetarian dishes that feature Plantain or 'Nendrakka' balls. The 'Sadyha' is often served for Onam (a harvest festival). And there are many more amazing recipes that I will get into later.

You may have noticed that Plantain is capitalised throughout the book, this is no typo my friends but a deliberate and intentional expression of the importance Plantain holds.

This book is an exploration of everything Plantain is and can be. In all its forms, wigs and outfits and the people and communities behind what makes it what it is. So for those of you who made it this far. Get ready to dive into serious Plantain-loving territory. For those of you who love the fruit as I do, I hope you will enjoy this as much as I enjoyed writing it. And I hope you take something with you.

1

MY LIFE AND PLANTAIN

So. It's a Saturday morning. Somewhere between Enfield and Barnet. I can tell it's still morning by looking outside my window. It's light outside. The birds are still chirping. And the raindrops from last night are still dripping down the concrete slabs that make up our flats and houses.

The sky is a powder blue and the clouds are a London white (not quite white but not quite grey either). Somewhere in-between. Spring looks like it's on the horizon, but any Londoner can see the subtle tinges of the 'pack an umbrella' hues hiding behind the clouds.

Down the road, an elderly woman sits patiently at the bus stop with her hands crossed on her laps and a trolley between her feet. Sharing the stop with her, a group of teenagers perform an orchestral symphony of London slang as she mutters inaudible curses.

Outside my door lie recycling bins that haven't been cleared for the third week in a row.

Looking past that, I stretch out my limbs and start my day. If my body could speak, it would say, 'damn. Here we go again.' Searching for a ray of hope, I open my laptop and load up Fruity Loops*. Hoping the melodies in my head from last

---

*   Also known as FL Studio, it is a digital audio workstation. It provides a graphical user interface with a pattern-based music sequencer that is used by users to create a wide range of audio projects.

night still come through. I stare assiduously at my screen for minutes that feel longer than they are. I press the keys on my keyboard and play. I play and play again until I give in to my lack of inspiration. I then do what any bored and uninspired person would do—I open up YouTube. I pause and eventually, I play Fela Kuti's 'Water No Get Enemy'. It reminds me that all great things can never be forced.

I move in synchronicity with the rhythms of Tony Allen as I make my way downstairs to the kitchen. My eyes scan the room for ingredients that can be of use. Past the bread, past the cereal and gbam! There it is.

As if by magic. The music from my speakers suddenly gets louder. Fela's saxophone solo fills the room and before I know it, I have a frying pan in my right hand, stainless steel knife in my left and two ripe Plantains in front of me. Now, I can start my day.

I know, it's a bit strange for someone to obsess about a fruit this much. I've often wondered if my love of Plantain hinted at something wrong within my wiring. In fact, when I first found out I had a 60,000 word count for this book, I thought, what could I possibly say? How many words can be said about Plantain? Even when I first approached this chapter, I was a bit lost. What personal relationship do I have with food? What does that even mean? Do I need to be diagnosed?

But then I started pacing down memory lane and piecing things together. Dot by dot. And you know what? It makes all the sense in the world. Because of course, I'm going to be writing about Plantain. Its splendid tastiness. Its resourcefulness. And its special place in the hearts of a global Plantain-loving community. For part of this book, like this chapter, I'm also going to be writing about myself. Because Plantain, along with just a few other things, has been at the heart of many of my life experiences.

'TO ME, THAT'S LIKE ASKING WHAT YOUR EARLY MEMORIES OF MILK OR WATER ARE. IT HAS ALWAYS JUST BEEN A PART OF LIFE.'
—RIAZ PHILLIPS

To track down where my Plantain craze began. I'd have to go back to the early days of my infancy. Back when the only nutrition I had access to was provided exclusively by Mum and the school dinner lady.

Even then, I wouldn't be able to pinpoint the exact moment that the Plantain floodgates were opened. Even after taking the time to think about it. Speaking to my mum, we still weren't too sure where it all began. With that being said, I've decided to pick a time and place where this story starts.

This takes me back to Sydney Road, Muswell Hill, North London. My family and I were one of the few Black families amidst a majority white working-class community. When it came to the other Black families on the estate, we didn't speak much but we shared a covert type of camaraderie.

My school was across the road from the estate. We had a small circle of gritty ground next to our flat with a 7ft wall that curved around the ground where we played 5 Alive football.

My mum was great at doing all kinds of braids and hair-styles. She would regularly do her friends' hair at our house. Through word of mouth, our humble abode became the closest thing to a Morris Roots the estate would ever see. Our house became a hub of activity. It wasn't just a Black house on the block, it felt like *the* Black house on the block.

One of the best things about living on the estate was my proximity to my friends. I vividly remember going over to friends' houses for dinners and sleepovers. Each house was different, each had a different character and a different smell. From all the home visits I made, one consistent theme remained etched in my memory. It was the food. More specifically, my unfamiliarity with my friends' family meals. Before being invited over for dinner. I had never seen or imagined smiley face potatoes with Heinz beans or spaghetti loops as dinner. I even saw chicken seasoned with ketchup!

The local shop in our area was owned by a South Asian family. The man who worked there used to call me 'Charlie'. I'm sure he knew what my name was. He knew my mother well enough. Although I think he was so used to calling all the other white kids by their English names that he gave me one too. The closest fast food shops to our house were either Chinese, Turkish or the 'fish n chips' shop. I remember riding our bikes in and around town, riding past countless faces that looked nothing like mine. Even in my friendship group, I stood out. As fun as my childhood in Muswell Hill was, the feeling of otherness was always there.

Okay. So what does this have to do with Plantain? Well, for me, Plantain became one of many important cultural reference points in my life. The food we ate at home was so different and unmistakably Black/African in comparison to everything I had experienced. A lot of my friends went home to bangers and mash, shepherd's pie and fish fingers etc. Don't get me wrong. I am no stranger to some Bird's Eye and McCain oven chips served on the days my mum was tired. Most of the time though, I came home to heavily seasoned meats and dense stews. Banana (Da Terra) E Peixe, Cachupa, or Calulu com Angu de Banana and more.

Dinner time for me looked and felt like an extension of our Blackness and our culture. Not only did I know we were culturally different from my friends, but I could taste it. Because of this, Plantain and other cultural foods were things I kept to myself. Like armour.

When I turned 10, we moved and my surroundings became more, to put it simply, Black. From Wood Green to Edmonton,

Burnt Oak and more. I started exploring areas where I had the ability to relate to people my age who were not just my cousins. Things started to change. My indifference to casual racism was replaced with intolerance. And a poor but well-meaning patois infused Yoruba twang that sat comfortably on my tongue.

Just like me, I would now see other Black kids express their cravings and love for Black foods, the same way I did. Including Plantain. My consumption of this fruit no longer needed to be a secret. Almost everyone else around me consumed it with the same vigour. It was the ultimate form of acceptance. At an age where fitting in with peers meant a great deal, it was a relief. I found comfort in seeing Plantain, palm-oil bottles and maggi cubes that weren't mine.

From then on, I would eat Black foods with conviction, anywhere and everywhere. From dishes out my mother's kitchen to foods that were from wider Black cultures, like Rice 'n' Peas, Jollof Rice and thick, palm oil stews.

I could lean into the fact that my fellow peers shared a similar appreciation for the fruit. Whether it was called Fried Plantin by my Caribbean pals. Dodo by my Nigerian friends. Banann by my Haitain buddies. Or Banana Frita by my PALOPS. We all knew to smile when we saw it coming out the pan and in box crates outside a shop.

When we look at Plantain in the scope of Black Britain, The civic and communal role that it plays cannot be quantified. Plantain, for me, and many others I'm sure, is one of the unifiers of Black identity within a very challenging Black Britain. Primarily due to the strong influence of the West African and Caribbean population in the UK. The experience of sharing tales of eating Plantain. Cooking

PLANTAIN
WORD
COUNT:
73

Plantain. Arguing about the correct pronunciation of Plantain. And all the above, provide a level of cultural intimacy within our community. It is one of the things that remind us how connected and together the Black diasporas are.

2

THE HISTORY
OF PLANTAIN

Plantain, like anything, has a history. A long and rich history spanning thousands of human years. Some early records show Plantain was enjoyed by people up to 5,000 BC in West Africa, in the highlands of New Guinea.[1]

That's more than 5,000 years of Plantain love in our earthly atmosphere. Yet despite its longstanding existence, the known and archived history of Plantain is scarce. The manner in which this glorious fruit's history has been recorded is scattered. Mentions of the fruit can be found in obscure and often inaccessible places. From lengthy academic journals with far too much higgi-hagga* to abstruse texts engulfed in the many histories of the slave trade. Even in these strange archival places, the social history of the fruit is never really accounted for. At least not in the way it should be. Instead, we find the social history of Plantain hanging in the balance of stories traded on dinner tables, parties and kitchen counters. As it often is for Black food cultures that have been extracted from their indigenous homes. Twisted, flipped, broken down and reconstructed for culinary appeal. Far from their endemic beginnings. Plantain falls victim to this archival failure and the way the history of the fruit has

---

* A term popularized by Patrick Obahiagbon, the former member of the House of Representatives of Nigeria, who used the term 'political higgi hagga', meaning text or speech that's as nonsensical as gibberish or mumbo jumbo.

been documented leaves a lot to be desired.

Before we remedy this and get into the history. First thing first. What even is Plantain?

Simply put, Plantain is a fruit. Specifically though, it's a berry. Yes, bananas and Plantains are actually berries. With their origins believed to be in Southeast Asia some thousands of years ago. They are part of the Musa family. The name for the genetic group that all bananas and Plantains come from. Unlike other fruits like oranges and apples, Plantain and bananas grow from herbaceous plants (plants with non-woody stems) that look like trees but are actually huge leaf stalks. Another feature associated with berries.

Both bananas and Plantains also develop from one single ovary but we can get into this later. What's most important to understand is that bananas and Plantains, despite looking very similar, are not the same. Again, for the people in the back, Plantains and bananas are not the same!

In the Musa family there are over 10 types of genetic variations called genomes. The world's most popular banana, the Cavendish, which is more commonly found in our super-markets, comes from the 'AAA' genome group. Plantain, for the most part, comes from the 'AAB' group. The 'A's and 'B's are a mixture of genetics from the ancestral Musa species. One called the Musa Acuminata and the other called Musa Balbisiana. The mix of the two birthed what would become the world's most favourite fruit. We'll get into exactly how that happened later. But the story goes. The banana, coming from the 'AAA' group, is softer, smaller and ready to eat raw. While Plantain coming from the 'AAB' group, is firmer, bigger and is best served cooked. Which is why it's also known as the 'cooking banana'.

Varieties found in fruits that come from the same family are common. Almost every fruit and vegetable has a range of cultivars. These are plant varieties that have been cultivated by way of selective breeding. For bananas and Plantains, there are over 100 cultivars. Selective breeding is practiced by agriculturalists in pursuit of particular characteristics in produce, using different agricultural methods.

For Plantains and bananas, our desired qualities are that they are strong enough to survive shipping, resist disease, insects, and most importantly, that they come without seeds. Believe it or not, one of the ancestral parents of both fruits, the Musa Balbisiana, came with seeds filling throughout the flesh, making them inedible.

Two of the most popular cultivars in the 'AAA' group have been the Gros Michel banana and the Cavendish banana. The Gros Michel being the first version of the soft, sweet and ready to eat banana that arrived in the West. Then, after dying out, it was taken over by the Cavendish banana, which are the dessert bananas we eat now. Called 'dessert' banana as it's more suitable for such, in direct contrast to the 'cooking' banana (Plantain).

In the 'AAB' group there are four main cultivars, known as the 'Plantain subgroup'. The French, French Horn, False Horn and Horn cultivars. Without the know-how it's hard to distinguish between the four. They all reaffirm the dichotomy between bananas and Plantains. The former being smaller, softer and eaten raw while the latter is otherwise cooked. However, there are also cultivars like the East African Highland Banana that belong in the 'AAA' group and possess the qualities of Plantains. They are eaten cooked, similar to Plantain but are not Plantains. Similarly the Saging Saba, mostly eaten in the Philippines, sits in the 'ABB' genome (a different genome entirely) but can be cooked like a baby-sized Plantain. These won't matter much to those of us in Europe and America where these cultivars aren't accessible. Still, I hope you're still with me.

The real history of Plantain starts with two words, tenacity and destiny.

Dan Koeppel, author of *Banana: The Fate of the Fruit That Changed the World*, explains that the journey of the Banana started with hundreds of varieties and over time (thousands of years to be exact), the amount of varieties declined dramatically and by the time the fruit reached Africa, they fell to single digits—*three*. Which means by the time the banana and its genetic family reached Africa from Southeast Asia, only a few species survived. Including, of course, Plantain.

First appearing in history books between 300–500 BC, Plantain is believed to have been introduced to East Africa from Southeast Asia by way of Subcontinent India and Papua New Guinea as early as 3000 BC. Traced back to Madagascar in 1000 BC and other regions in West Africa between 1000–5000 BC[2].

The journey of Plantain is then understood to have travelled from Africa, to the Caribbean in the 1500s[3]. Then, 500+ years later, in a frying pan inside the kitchen of my North London residence in 2021.

The timeline of Plantain is easier traced through the history of its trade and domestication. Starting with the ancient Greek records of Alexander the Great's campaign to

India in 327 BC[4]. Some scholars still debate whether these stories are accurate but it is mostly accepted.

Looking at other sources of information. The etymology of a word can also serve some sort of indication of its history and origin. For example, the word 'apple', formerly spelled æppel in Old English, derives from the Proto-Germanic root 'aplaz', taking you through a whole bunch of Indo-European histories, including Norse mythology where the fruit is heavily featured.

Using the etymology of the words 'banana' and 'Plantain', things are slightly more difficult. Supposedly, the word banana takes us back to Africa. One story being that the word originates from the Arabic word for 'Banan' meaning fingertips. Which in a way describes the shape of a banana bunch. Another story is that the word 'banana' is taken directly from Wolof[*]. The native language of Wolof people across Senegal and Gambia, where 'banana' is understood to mean five-toed.

But none of this takes us as far back as we need to understand Plantain's story in Africa. Arabic banana traders only appear in the history books for how they moved across Southeast Asia. The Wolof people and the use of their language is only properly archived after encounters with the Portuguese after the 15th century. Similarly, the etymology of the word Plantain, doesn't take us as far back as we want to either. The Spanish term for Plantain, which is Plátano, is believed to be derived from 'Palatana' or 'Balatana', the apparent Kalinago word for banana. The Kalinago language is spoken by the Kalinago people, also known as Island Caribs, who, along with Arawakans, were two main indigenous groups from the Lesser Antilles (smaller islands across the Caribbean sea), for whom the history only appears after the Spanish arrived in the

---

[*]   Wolof is a language spoken in parts of Senegal, Gambia and Mauritania, which is the native language of the Wolof people

Caribbean. 'Plátano' also relates to the word for the Spanish Plane Tree 'Plantanus', which Spanish conquistadors thought looked like Plantain plants. Again, neither of these links tells us what was happening with the fruit between its journey from Southeast Asia to Africa and Africa to the Caribbean.

In Judith Carney's book *In the Shadow of Slavery*, she explores the fact that there are other potential origins of the fruit's name. For example Plantain, she states, could have derived its name from the word 'Koba' that means plant in São Tomé and other Southeast African countries[5]. So maybe to understand more about the fruit's journey in Africa we would have to start looking at all the other names for Plantain on the continent, particularly among tribal dialects. For example, some early mentions of Plantain include the 1978 release of *The Cambridge History of Africa*, edited by J.D Fage, which states that Plantain was mentioned 'under the name of avalaneeyra in the island of São Tomé[6]' in 1506 by Portuguese printer Valentim Fernandes. But with the word Plantain itself, we are still at odds.

When we look towards Plantain's journey from Africa to the Caribbean, however, we start to get a much clearer picture.

Thomas Nicolas, who served as a translator for the Levant Company, a English chartered company in the 1500s, archived his first time encountering Plantain in 1526 in São Tomé and said the below, which I've translated from tapped* English (feel free to read the original transcript *In the Shadow of Slavery: Africa's Botanical Legacy in the Atlantic World* by Judith A. Carney and Richard Nicholas Rosomoff):

'The Island (São Tomé) has good wine and all sorts of fruits, potatoes, melons, pears, apples, oranges, lemons, pomegranates, figs, peaches and many others, but none of them hit

---

*   A term describing something or someone that is beyond understanding. 'That's tapped' or 'He/she is tapped'.

like Plantain. It grows from a tree but has no timber (wood) in it. It grows upwards with thick marvelous leaves that are almost two yards long and almost half a yard broad. The tree only yields once and it is cut down, in whose place another one springs and continues. The fruit grows on a branch, and every tree yields two or three of those branches. Some bear more and some bear less. Some forty, some thirty. When it is ripe it is Black and in eating, more delicate than any conserve'.[7]

Side note, could São Tomé's visibility in Plantain's archival history explain my obsession with it? Who knows. But more importantly, in Nicholas's original quote, he reflects on the formation of a Plantain tree from its sucker (its root) to its fruits. First, he explains that the tree is technically not a tree as it has no wood in it. Remember that Plantain like other Musa species do not grow from trees but from herbaceous perennials (herbaceous stems) called 'succulent stems', also known as a pseudostem. The pseudostem grows from the bottom part of the plant buried underneath the soil, also called the corm, that is located where the roots are. From the corm, the pseudostem shoots up from the ground like a stalk, with tight leaf sheaths spiralling around it. It grows, and grows taller, dropping off dead leaves and eventually, the stalk emerges and starts leaning, pushing itself out from the pseudostem and producing a beautifully elegant-looking flower. The flower, called an inflorescence, is usually coloured—a mix of purple and very rouge tones that bears the fruits—and in this case would be Plantain.

Nicholas notes the leaves of the Plantain plant are big and thick. These same leaves can be used for a variety of purposes, most notably for cooking or serving food on. This gives life to a theory that it was a Plantain leaf Adam and Eve had covered themselves in, giving Plantain biblical significance.

But don't hold me to that. Amongst the many interesting features of Plantain is the manner in which the fruit can be produced, something that Nicholas also notes in his bulgy quote. Referring back to my mention of the sucker, which is what the root of the plant is called, before the Plantain plant blooms, the sucker can be transplanted to grow new Plantain plants elsewhere. Literally taking it and planting it a couple meters away to birth a clone of the previous plant. This is what we call vegegative propagation. It's a process of plant reproduction that allows for a Plantain 'tree' planted 20 years ago to still bear fruit till this day. Finally, Nicholas mentions that when the Plantain is ripe and at its blackest, it is the tastiest, referring to the ripest stage of Plantain, where the skin is black and the starches have converted to sugars, giving truth to the phrase: 'the blacker the berry, the sweeter the juice'.

As I mentioned earlier, Plantain's usage is expansive. In various colonial plantain-tions throughout the Caribbean around the 1500s, the Portuguese and Spanish developed markets for both bananas and Plantain. Here, Plantains were employed for a few things. The first use was as a valuable intercropping plant. Intercropping is a practice where more than one crop is grown on the same field at the same time. Done to produce a greater crop yield than if the land was used for one crop.

Another use of Plantain on colonial plantations was due to the towering leaves that the Plantain plant produced. These leaves were used to shade and protect valued items. Plantains and bananas were also relied upon to feed slave populations due to their nutritional value.[8]

Still, much of the documented information we have about Plantain is disappointing. Dutch writer and ethnobotanist Gerda Rossel's *Taxonomic-linguistic study of Plantain in Africa* published in 1998 stated:

'Where musa is concerned, archaeological evidence is absent and written sources are scarce. Unlike archaeology and history, however, botany and agronomy are based on present-day material, which is plentiful. This living material may serve, if well interpreted, as a window to the past. The study of (the spread of) crop names in languages provides an alternative source of information. These disciplines therefore play an important part in such a combined approach of Plantain history in Africa.'[9] Rossel is right. There is plenty of botanical information available on Plantain and the rest of the Musa family. But there's more to the fruit's story of the fruit than this. As observed in Thomas Nicholas's diary, Plantain has for the most part been noted in the history books due to its botanical makeup and the way it is cultivated rather than its societal and anthropological value.

PLANTAIN WORD COUNT: 147

THE SCIENCE OF IT ALL

The botanical crinkum crankum* that explains what Plantain is differs from what most people understand Plantain to be. Plantain, as mentioned, belongs to the 'AAB' genome group Musa species. The Musa species, more accurately termed 'Musa genera', belongs to the Musaceae family of flowering plants. The scientific name for the genetic group that most of our bananas and Plantains belong in. Along with Musa, there are two other genera that belong to the Musaceae family—the

---

* A term, also popularized by Patrick Obahiagbon, having a similar meaning to 'Higga Hagga'. Something too complicated or nonsensical to be understood.

Musella Lasiocarpa and the Ensete. The Musella Lasiocarpa produces a single fruit, the Chinese dwarf banana and the Ensete produces what's called a false banana. It's labelled false because it does not actually produce any fruit. Though the majority of the plant is still used for food in parts of countries like Ethiopia. Neither the Lasiocarpa nor the Ensete produce as many cultivars as the Musa genera. Are you still following?

With the Musa genera, over 70 species are known. And no category is as important as the Musa Acuminata and Musa x Paradisiaca. This sounds quite complex, but it's fairly simple to explain. I hope. The Musa Acuminata, one of the earliest domesticated species of bananas, is the parent to most of the modern edible dessert bananas we eat today, like the Cavendish bananas and Gros Michel. Interestingly, its earliest sibling, the Musa Balbisiana, is better known for being the 'wild' banana, because it carries seeds. These are bananas that carry hard, black, distinguished seeds all throughout their mushy flesh. As a result, they are classed as inedible.

Through what can only be described as divine intervention, some thousands of years ago, Musa Acuminata fused with Musa Balbisiana to create new hybrid subsets of Musa cultivars, known as Musa x Paraisiaca. These new hybrids are where we find most of our edible bananas and Plantains.

As a result, the Plantain cultivars as well as the banana cultivars became what we call triploids. What on earth is a triploid? I hear you say. Triploids describe Plantains and bananas that have three copies of each chromosome (as opposed to two) that hold their genes from the Musa Acuminata and the Musa Balbisiana. The Cavendish banana 'AAA', and the Plantain 'AAB'.

Because of this, they cannot reproduce sexually because their chromosomes cannot be equally divided to make a sex cell. This triploid characteristic resulted in a range of fruits that took both the qualities of the Musa Balbisiana and the edible nature of the Musa Acuminata to produce new fruits. Fruits that provided new culinary experiences. In other words, this is the marriage our beautiful Plantain crops were created in.

Remember when I said 'the botanical crinkum crankum that explains exactly what Plantain is, differs from what most people understand to be Plantain to be'? This refers to what botanists call 'true Plantains'. True Plantains are cultivars from the 'AAB' group that share the qualities we are all used to Plantains having. Being less sweet, fatter, starchier and able to be used in a variety of cooking processes. But not all Musa species that are considered Plantains are actually 'true Plantains'. Similarly, there are Musa species that aren't actually Plantains but possess the characteristics of 'true Plantains'.

For example, the East African Highland Banana (EAHB), most popular in Uganda. The EAHB acts like a Plantain, cooks like a Plantain, even looks like a Plantain and if it were available in a market stall you'd probably mistake it for a Plantain. But it actually sits in the same biological genome group as a Cavendish banana as an 'AAA' triploid.

Similarly, there are cultivars that come from the 'AAB' triploid Plantain group that are nothing like 'true Plantains'. One such cultivar is the Latundan Banana, sometimes referred to as the 'silk banana' or the 'apple banana' and is popular in the Philippines. It is a cultivar that botanically speaking is a Plantain. But in terms of its appearance and cooking possibility, it's a lot more like a dessert banana. Being that it is smaller and softer and ready to eat raw. Latundan is not the only banana within the 'AAB' genome group to share these qualities. Which is why in different parts of the world, Plantains are sometimes called bananas and vice versa. But it's safe to make the global distinction that bananas are the softer, smaller, ready to eat berries and Plantains are the ones you cook! So no stress.

Now I'd like to get away from the nitty-gritty sciencey stuff because my own brain is tiring. But before I do, I would like to address a small faction of society that believes that because Plantain is a hybrid fruit it is therefore unnatural (yes they exist!).

Given the rise of GMO foods and its hysteria, the association hybrid foods have with Dexter's laboratories is understandable. Double-headed chickens, ducks with two beaks, the Belgian Blue, otherwise known as the Supercow, and seedless grapes.

I get it. Processed foods really are the enemy. And most GMO foods are, in truth, a bit dodgy, but genetically modified foods aren't always the product of a dishonest process. For one, foods can genetically modify naturally, in fact they often do. In the case of Plantain, this is exactly what happened. Thousands of years ago, the Musa Acuminata and the Musa Balbisiana, came together like a glitch in the system. Making what is technically, a hybrid. But that's the natural part! What happened after that was humans capitalizing on finally being able to eat these yellow fruits through marketing and global business.

When it comes to hybrid plants and cultivars, there's a symbiotic relationship between agriculturalists and genetic engineering. Plantains and bananas don't disperse seeds. They have none to begin with. The only reason Plantains and bananas grow the way they do is because they have been domesticated by way of calculated cultivation by human hands thousands of years ago. So there's that.

AFRICA

As we have seen, the story of Plantain is one where the science of it serves as an access point into its history. And even though bananas and the general Musa species are thought to originate from the Southeast Asian-Pacific region[10], the diversity of Plantain cultivars and varieties of the fruit, are the highest in, wait for it… AFRICA.

A cornerstone in African cuisine and its socioeconomic value across different groups across the continent. It's only right that Africa is home to the most diverse varieties of the fruit. In West and Central Africa, selective breeding and vegetative propagation have diversified the types of Plantain introduced to the continent. Phytoliths, which are microscopic structures found in plant tissue long after the plant has died, can be used to evidence this. Thanks to phytoliths we have been able to trace Plantains as early as the 1st millennium BC in south Cameroon[11]—the wows of modern science.

Shrouded in mystery, Africa is often footnoted in Plantain's history. As a location that connects Southeast Asia to Latin America, rather than a subject of inquiry.

So, let's talk a little more about the beautiful continent that is Africa and its beautiful marriage to the beautiful fruit that is Plantain. In 1485 it is understood that the Portuguese established a sugar colony in São Tomé[12]. Let's also take a moment to appreciate the consistent mentions of São Tomé, which are giving me life. Mentions of São Tomé in literature, art and music are rare, I always get stunned whenever I come across them. Hence us taking a moment. Thank you. Carrying on. The story goes that from the 1470's the Bantu-speaking people of West-Central Africa would be in contact with the

Portuguese mariners.[13] Ten points for the person who knows what the dietary staple of the Bantu-speaking people of West-Central Africa was? Yep. That is right, none other than Plantain.[14]

So when the Portuguese came to São Tomé in the second half of the 15th century, they were exposed to cultures across the Guinea coast including countries like Senegal and Gambia where Wolof people are recorded to have lived. This would explain the Portuguese adoption of the word 'banana' for Plantain, which we established before may have come from the Wolof language. And of course, the Portuguese had a strong presence in this region during the formative period of the Atlantic slave trade.[15]

This story is further propagated by Judith Carney's mention of 'Koba'. Used as a name for Plantain in São Tomé and other names for Plantain throughout Africa before the Portuguese arrived.[16]

Now as much as I'd like to claim Plantain was introduced to the world via São Tomé and trust me I really would. There is far more to the history of Plantain within Africa we simply don't know. Much about Plantain

DID YOU KNOW THE PLANTAIN DIVERSITY IN THE DRC IS ONE OF THE HIGHEST IN AFRICA?[1]

culture that exists today seems to mirror and come directly from culinary and agricultural practices originating in Africa.

In Gerda Rossel's *Taxonomic Linguistic study of Plantain in Africa*, Rossel asserts that 'no satisfying explanation' has been given for the diversity and the amount of Plantain variations in Africa[17]. But still a whopping $120\approx$ cultivars have been found in Africa, which is a huge amount and approximately 10 times the amount discovered in Asia.[18]

As early as 3000 BC, Plantain was a cultivar crucial to the

expansion of Bantu people* throughout the Central African rainforest[19]. Substantiating a vital history of cultivation and propagation of Plantain in Africa that was essential for its journey from the Asian-Pacific through to the Caribbean. As opposed to having simply passed through the region.

In Nigeria, for example, the presence of Plantain is understood to go far back. In Sonpie Kpone-Tonwe's paper 'The Historical Tradition of Ogoni', she states that in Ogoni villages (home to the Ogoni people, a group in Nigeria going back as far 15 BC) shrines honour their deity with yams and Plantain. Kpone-Tonwe reveals that this practice is believed to have its roots dating back to Nama, a pre-colonial area in Northeast Nigeria.[20] In this region, Plantain was even used as a ritualistic fruit for ancestral spirits and ancient Gods.[21]

CARIBBEAN AND LATIN AMERICA

The Caribbean, extending to parts of Latin America, is another region that also has an interesting history with Plantain. A staple food for a cluster of nations within the Caribbean, the continent is home to a wide range of culinary methods. Creating a unique and rich blend of Plantain cultures. In Latin America, Peru and Colombia sit in the top 10 producers of Plantain, with Colombia ranking quite high in fourth place.[22] Ecuador, Costa Rica, Guatemala, Peru and Panama all sit in the top 15 exporting countries of the fruit.[23]

In a research paper conducted by Douglas H. Marin, Turner B. Sutton and Kenneth R. Barker, they reveal there are actually studies of pre-Columbian graves in Peru where remnants of Plantain were found[24]. So once again, the history of Plantain could possibly pre-date what we think we know

---

* Bantu people have been recorded to be in Africa as early as 3000 BC, migrating throughout the continent towards Southern Africa in 500 BC.

when it comes to the fruit. In the same research paper, it is stated that the Musa family may have been a major food crop in tropical South America for over 2,000 years.[25]

Like in West Africa, Latin America also suffers from lack-lustre archival data. Nevertheless the story of Plantain in the Caribbean starts with a man named Fray Tomas de Berlanga. Fray Tomas de Berlanga was the fourth bishop of Panama. The bishop was born in Spain in the 1500s and is known for many things. Namely, solving a famed dispute between Spanish conquistadors, Francisco Pizzaro and Diego de Almagro over a division of territory.

On his list of notable achievements is his transportation of a particular crop from the Canary Islands to the Dominican Republic[26].

Amongst the botanical crew there is no real consensus on how the banana species reached the Canary Islands. Some suspect the Portuguese, after explorating the Gulf of Guinea, between 1469–1474[27], were the ones to bring the banana to the islands. Others, however, believe it arrived later than that, supposedly from the Philippines, which during the 1400s and early 1500s was under Spanish control[28].

It is believed that in 1516, Berlanga took with him, from the Canary Islands, Plantain and banana clones to Santo Domingo[29]. Ushering it, officially into the New World.

The Spanish had started their expansion throughout the region in the Caribbean around 1490 and were in search of gold and other riches. Legend has it that a Spanish conquistador called Bernal Díaz del Castillo of the early 1500s made an admission and stated, 'we went there to serve God, and also to get rich.'[30]

The arrival of Plantain and its method of vegetative propagation, combined with the tropical conditions of the

Caribbean, produced an opportunity[31]. The result would be, the upstart of a plantation economy that would oversee millions of Africans enslaved. Hauled over from a mix of West African communities to the Caribbean via the transatlantic slave routes.[32] Indigineous tribes would be pushed out of their ancestral lands in favour of large colonial operations and commercial activity. The remaining communities would be forced into native slavery, alongside indentured servants hauled from differents backgrounds.[33] With the arrival of Britain in the centuries to come, the make-up of plantation workers ranged from Pre-Columbian, West African, Irish and Southeast Asian.

Berlanga, along with other expansionists, went on to plant the banana species in various nations. Haciendas, which were physical spaces that formed plantation economies, factories and mines were placed across the Caribbean regions and Latin America, contributing to the creation of hybrid and creolized cultures.[34]

In 1652, Heinrich von Uchteritz of German nobility, was captured by England and sold to a planter in Barbados. Don't ask me how, or why. He described one of the houses of the enslaved Africans on the island mentioning, that they were, 'built of inferior wood, almost like dog huts, and covered with leaves from trees which they call Plantain, which is very broad and almost shelf-like, and serves very well against rain.'[35]

Plantain, considering its ease of propagation in such climates, was routinely used and relied on by slaves and poor communities,[36] extending to indentured servants long after the abolition of slavery.

In former Spanish colonies, however, including those in Latin America, Plantain continued to gain prominence in the region's many diets. From the Dominican Republic to Peru, dishes like Mofongo (DC) or Bollitos de Plátano (Venez) were commonly made.

The cultural significance is further observed with the figure of the 'Jibaro'. Becoming a national symbol of pride in parts of Puerto Rico, and particularly in the countryside, the Jibaro, commonly featured in images and portrayal with Plantains as fruits of labour, wasn't always an appreciated figure. Much like 'jornaleros', which translates 'labourers', they were viewed as victims of the Spanish colonial government. During the early periods of Spanish colonialism, anti-colonialist attitudes spread over the country. The Jibaro was eventually viewed in a positive light because he was independent and autonomous, working for himself and being happy with little.[37]

So when sentiments towards fighting colonial rule and imperialism became popular, so did the idea of the Jibaro, a figure totally abstract from any allure of Spanish rule. Of course, by association and possibly by destiny, the Plantain followed suit. Becoming a delicacy that went from mere slavery food, to a food associated with 'the people', freedom and all things that make a 'good' honest person. Not only in Puerto Rico but across the region.

The journey of Plantain within the Caribbean has been impacted by difficult trade agreements too. The agricultural economy is an important part of the prosperity of these former plantation economies. In 1976, the Lomé convention came into play. A trade agreement between the European Economic Community (EEC) and the African, Caribbean and Pacific (ACP) that came about to ease new frameworks of cooperation between EEC and ACP nations. It would allow agricultural and mineral exports to enter the EEC free of duty, meaning, the plantation economies that weren't part of Central America's lasting Banana Republic legacy could still rely on exporting bananas and of course, Plantains.[38]

However, as the saying goes, 'all good things come to an

end.' In 1995, just two years after Bill Clinton entered the White House, the United States government petitioned to the World Trade Organisation (WTO), suggesting that the agreements between the two parties were incompatible with WTO regulations and stating that all preferential trade agreements between the EEC and ACP should stop.[39]

As a result, countries like Jamaica suffered from the decline of the industry. And with agriculture being such a large section of the economy at the time, this resulted in wider socio-economic effects. Later, in 2003, the Cotonou Agreement came into force, which provided similar advantages for ACP countries.[40]

THE BATTLE OF THE MUSAS: WHY THE BANANA AND NOT THE PLANTAIN?

I mentioned before that the banana cultivar most of us are used to eating is the Cavendish banana. Most of us don't know anything else. But before the Cavendish, there was a former cultivar that reigned supreme as the first dessert banana introduced to the 'world'. And by world I mean, Europe and America, like in Marvel movies. The Gros Michel became one of the first and more important tropical crops fueling the plantation economies for centuries to come.

The Gros Michel is a cultivar which was wiped out by the Panama disease in the 1950s, and was replaced by the Cavendish banana—the most dominant and famous banana cultivar. The Gros Michel and Cavendish varieties would go on to have huge significance both economically and culturally in one of the most prolific regions in the world. North America, specifically the USA and Canada.

The popularity of the banana started with Samuel Zemurray, also known as 'Sam the Banana Man', an American entrepreneur who is credited for the banana boom (to put it mildly). In the late 1800s, early 1900s, a young Samuel Zemurray first started selling close to over-ripe bananas to grocery store owners on the Illinois Central Railroad train just after 1893 when he first came across what would become a tropical sensation in Alabama.

At the time bananas, believe it or not, were relatively unknown, viewed by those who did know it as a rare exotic fruit. Much of this was attributed to the fact that refrigerated shipping across international waters wasn't widely accessible. So a young and determined Zemurray eventually moved on to take over the controversial United Fruit Company. Turning the banana, from an unknown fruit, into a household and supermarket staple.

For Plantain, however, there was a different trajectory. Instead of being featured in commercials like the banana, or existing in mainstream folklore or having its own cartoon characters dressed up in pyjamas and despite its prominence in the early settlements of plantations across the Caribbean, Latin American, Europe and America, Plantain stayed relatively unknown.

Zemurray and his company, the United Fruit Company, took over national markets to build them into what has been dubbed 'banana republics'. A term used to describe a politically unstable country dependent upon the exportation of a limited-resource product.

At the height of United Fruits Company's success in the 1920s, with help from strong influences like the CIA, the company went on to politically influence the occupation of Latin American land for the production of bananas (we will get into this more in another chapter). It was clear that they were the driving force for mass banana markets across Europe and America. Without them, who knows if the banana would have populated the world the way it did. Who knows, Americans and Brits could have been waking up and adding fried Plantain to their pancakes instead. So why wasn't it? What stopped Plantain peels from being slipped on in Charlie Chaplin comedy sketches? Or Plantain in pyjamas becoming a bonafide hit amongst the kids?

Well, one reason is the difference in taste between the Plantain and other members of the Musa family. In early documentations of Plantain, it was always noted that Plantain is less sweet in comparison to dessert bananas like the Cavendish. Plantains only release ethene gas (a process that allows starches to convert into sugars) when they are Black as opposed to when yellow like bananas. As a result it doesn't easily qualify as a quick go to snack like a banana does. To me of course, Plantain is the sweetest ting of life, but I suppose if you peel a Plantain and try to eat it raw the sweetness and ease of eating would pale in comparison to a banana. So maybe it was never Plantain's destiny to be a mainstream delicacy like the Cavendish banana.

Across slave quarters and working-class communities, Plantain became an important nutrient for both its consumers and plantation owners who needed a cheap and nutritious way to feed their workers all throughout the year. Cooked for dinner, lunch and even breakfast, going on to become an essential part of the region's cuisine. Judith Carney underpins this in *In the Shadow of Slavery: Africa's Botanical Legacy in the Atlantic World* where she states, 'a profitable commerce in human beings required sources of surplus food to feed slaves en route to the Americas... In the wetter regions, Plantains and the African groundnut dominated food supplies'.[41] In particular, 'Plantains frequently provisioned slave ships leaving tropical Africa.'[42]

Over time, Plantain and the dessert banana have taken very different trajectories. Bananas being offered into the culinary world stripped from its slightly tropical context to be redefined into an article of Western culture. Efforts have helped transform their significance in the world, from British comedy skits and American idioms, to $120,000 contemporary art talking points[43]. Europe and North America have embraced the banana with open arms and rebranded it as theirs.

In comparison, Plantain is the uglier duckling with its history of antiquity in Africa amiss. Plantain seemed to not pass the test of mainstream eligibility. With its very direct association with slavery, the disenfranchised and Afro-Caribbean cuisine, Plantain in the context of Black food history, and food history in general, can be seen as a symbol of the anti-colonial sentiment.

THE PLANTAIN REPUBLIC: PEOPLE AND PLANTAIN

Okay. So we go again. Another chapter in my extended love letter to Plantain. The crown jewel of the Musa family. The peng one in the group. The incessant joy of my life. Carefully forged from the philosopher's stone. Plantain-type beat. The true elixir of life. The only product I don't mind throwing all my money at. (Alexa, play 'Chop My Money' by P-Square). £1 for 3? £2 for 3? £3, £4, £5? I will pay it all.

The community of Plantain lovers or, as I like to call them, the Plantain Republic is strong and large in numbers. From Black British kitchens all over the UK to dining rooms 4,000+ miles away in Kinshasa. People far and wide are all hoarding, frying, double-frying, roasting, boiling, baking, mashing and enjoying the delicacy that is Plantain. The Plantain Republic rep* the fruit anywhere they go. They put it on T-shirts, they have Plantain-themed parties, they write books about it (ahem) and so much more. Members of the Plantain Republic are reading this book nodding their heads and even clicking their fingers, I would know, as I, too, am a member.

The Plantain Republic are passionate and protective when it comes to the fruit. We aren't always united (see Chapter 4: Plantain vs Plant-in), but when it comes to protecting the honour of our Plantain, our unity prevails.

---

* Represent

The community's passion is perhaps best shown through Black British internet history. Not too long ago, in the far away land of Instagram, 2019. There was a Plantain scandal that had me and my fellow members in the Plantain Republic in shock. Without going into the details of it all, it was a classic case of food gentrification. A white-owned company created a 'vegan' Plantain brand, the type that gets stocked at your favourite, or least favourite, organic supermarket. As these things go, this brand won a food award and was widely praised for being innovative for their creation of Plantain crisps. Of course, we, the Plantain Republic, knew that Plantain crisps were not new at all. Upon discovering the news, Black British Twitter took charge and had a say. The brand received an onslaught of thunder and holy ghost fire in the form of insta comments and tweets. Whilst the comments were aimed at this specific brand, they were also reflective of our feelings towards the nature of food gentrification and how it can work to diminish cultural heritage, history and ownership.

For those of you who, whilst reading this book are wondering if you qualify for membership into the Plantain Republic, here is a checklist.

YOU ARE A MEMBER OF THE PLANTAIN REPUBLIC IF:

- If you instinctively make note of where you see Plantain stockists and add it to your Plantain mental map.
- If you love partaking in debates about the best

way to cook Plantain.

- If secretly you get a thrill from dodging the oil that pops as you fry Plantain.
- If eating Plantain makes you dance.
- If you sporadically tweet about Plantain for no real reason.
- If you feel passionately about the manner in which Plantain should be cut.
- If you have bought a Plantain-themed item including but not limited to a T-shirt, mug, journal, pen, poster, phone case, etc.

Despite the strong and visible community of the Plantain Republic, Plantain still feels like a secret delicacy that most are not familiar with. The unfamiliarity that society has with the fruit is probably why time and time again, year after year, meal after meal, portion after portion, someone asks me, 'What kind of banana are you eating?'

Societally, Plantain is a fruit that is at the crux of many 'diverse' communities. Namely Black British communities and other immigrant communities. In fact, if you wanted an indicator of where ethnic communities reside in London, you could probably do so by locating where Plantain is sold. I can always tell what my proximity to a Black or otherwise ethnic community is when I see bowls or boxes of ripe Plantains outside the local corner shops. That's not to say there aren't Black people where there isn't Plantain. But when you do find a corner shop with Plantain crates, you're probably not far.

HUMANS AND FOOD

For those of us growing up in the UK, the genesis of the Plantain craze that sustains us now rested firmly on the shoulders of the older generation that first immigrated here. Although traces of Black British communities and even Black cuisine have existed in Britain for centuries, it was the wave of Black Caribbeans first immigrating into the island in the 50s and 60s that would go on to create a Black food sub-economy. For Plantain, it was the Caribbean restaurants and market stalls in Cardiff, London, Bristol and more, that sold us portions of the fruit for as much as you could get fried chips for. The aunties and uncles that drove their vans to and from their wholesalers to stock Plantain in our local corner shops. It's been 26 years and I'm still yet to see Plantain stocked in my closest big chain supermarket.

Food has been and always will be a cultural expression and a visceral way of maintaining home and culture. For travelling communities, food allows them to pass down cultural troves to their children, who they are raising in a new and often alien land. Sometimes used to battle against spaces that work to ostracise, food is deeper than what we digest for enjoyment. Food, for us, is actually an important part of navigating our hyphenated British identities. During my childhood, in a white working-class community, I clinged onto my mum's food like Captain America's shield in the face of spaghetti letters and smiley potatoes. No offence. Furthermore, without the various corner shop uncles I've called bossman over the years and high street eateries—from the Brown Eagles in Woodgreen, Tom's Kitchen in Hackney Central, Jay Dee's Catering in Ladbroke Grove and all the other spots I've exchanged my pennies for Plantain, I wouldn't be writing this book. Proud and loud food culture is a symbol of resistance and cultural strength in a society that does not seek to embrace our multifaceted identities.

YOUTHFUL PLANTAIN EXPRESSION

Many generations have been guided by the gift of Plantain. They have passed it onto their children and their children have passed it onto their children. Of all the generations of Plantain lovers, however, no one has created such a globalised and expansive network of ardent Plantain enthusiats like the millennials and Gen Zers.

PLANTAIN WORD COUNT: 280

A simple 'Plantain' search on Twitter would lead you into a wormhole with hundreds of Twitter accounts either spewing Plantain appreciation tweets or naming their social media accounts after Plantain, and often doing both. Whether it's somebody responding to the coronavirus pandemic by praying that they 'never see a sickness that stops them from tasting Plantain' or thousands of accounts naming themselves PlantainPapi, PlantainMami or even PlantainGovernor in dedication to the glorious fruit.

Even Gen Z YouTubers like Ronzo and FOKTV can be found travelling around Stratford shopping centre asking the general public the perennial question of our time ,'how do you pronounce Plantain?'

Black Twitter has bred Plantain-themed parties, Plantain themed T-shirts, mugs and pens—really all we are waiting for is a Plantain-inspired mixtape.

There is even a zine named *Plantain Papers* that centers the voices, stories and experiences of Plantain eaters around the world in a yearly independent journal. The publication stands as an example of the multifaceted ways Plantain intersects the congregation of community as a horticultural-cultural glue.

And I just have to mention. Prior to reading *Plantain Papers* I never thought Plantain could ever be an agent for romance. But in *Plantain Papers* issue 001, there was Tahirah Edwards-Byfield's comical and genius dating filtration system. Where she filters through potential dating partners by asking them the very important question of how they feel about Plantain. It made total sense. I had to ask myself, could I really build a life with someone who doesn't smile at the sight of Plantain like I do?

Plantain Papers, like the other aforementioned manifestations of love for Plantain, are examples of how we and future generations continue to establish the profound cultural relevance of Plantain, despite mainstream platforms overlooking it. Even if we never get to see our sentiments about Plantain reflected in mainstream media and forever have to produce our own publications, events and platforms to show appreciation. Calm. We'll never get tired of it. It's a love that sustains itself.

Now, if you are not a self professed member of the Plantain Republic you might find me to be extreme in my love of the fruit. But if I haven't convinced you that I'm not insane, here are some other people who also share my passion. It's not just me!

First on my list of people from the Plantain Republic is Christian Adofo. Christian is a writer, cultural producer and is also a member of the *A Quick Ting On* family. Writing his first book from the series, called *A Quick Ting On Afrobeats*. Before all of that however, Christian was a lover of Plantain. The fruit was introduced to him through his parents and extended family as well as at Ghanaian hall parties where Plantain was regularly served.

When I asked Christian what his fondest memory of Plantain was, he told me: 'It would most probably be at home on most Saturday afternoons where my parents would cook, and once you heard the fizz of oil in the kitchen you would immediately know Plantain was in the frying pan.'

Christian goes on to explain that when he hears the term 'Plantain culture' he thinks of 'enjoyment. A prelude for people to relax around food which is nourishing and well-seasoned (in direct contrast to the culinary offerings of Babylonia). Ultimately it's a social ritual which makes you connect to something bigger than yourself and there is no hierarchy.'

See, it isn't just me.

On the topic of food gentrification, Christian raises some important points asserting, 'There is an uneasy relationship with food from Black communities and the first arrivals into those areas which are changing, appropriating those ingredients. We have seen it through these pop up markets that are branded under the 'street food' label and I find it problematic. As existing restaurants and shops sell ingredients and food at an affordable price for the loyal locals yet the newcomers pride themselves on 'locally sourcing' produce and very often gas up the health benefits of foods that are unknown to them. So this new intake of white middle-class people see it as a luxury superfood and not recognizing it's part of staple diet for the existence of Black working-class communities. Thus, the prices of Plantain and other foods become inflated and the only people who can comfortably afford the food are the same ones who can have a choice between caviar or callaloo, leading uncle or auntie to travel further away from their high street market to cop the food which has always nourished them and made them feel a sense of home away from their ancestral one.'

As a member of the Plantain Republic, Christian, like many of us, takes the cooking of Plantain seriously. In fact on the topic of cooking, Christian explains: 'Making food is a form of therapy for me. I can put a good DJ mix on for two to three hours in the background to ground myself and take my time to prepare the ingredients and experiment as I go along making a meal. The best food is made with care and love and in the last five years I have enjoyed cooking not only for myself but for other people.'

My final question to Christian is a tough one, but he answers it like a champ.

'You are tasked with proving how amazing Plantain is to someone who's never had it before, how do you do it?'

'Two ways. Plantains must be hella "solar eclipse", ripe skinned (black). I will either top and tail the Plantain and make a slit down the middle leaving the skins on. Then use a fork to prick the Plantain and let it boil for 10-15 minutes in a pan of lightly salted water until the Plantain skin falls off to make some sweet steamed ones.

The alternative is to get some ripe Plantains. Top and tail again. Peel the skin away and cut the Plantain in half length-ways. Marinate in all purpose seasoning, honey and fresh lime juice for 20 mins. Preheat the oven to 170 C° and then wrap the Plantains in foil. Place in the oven for 10-15 mins or until the Plantain caramelizes and take out to H'enjooooy!'

CHRISTIAN'S ABSOLUTE NO-GO

In his own words is, 'tomato ketchup. If you ever see a bottle of the red stuff near a golden boomerang (Plantain) just launch it like a javelin out a window.'

For my next chat, I have another member of the Plantain Republic, who goes by the name of Ifeyinwa Frederick. Co-founder of London-based Nigerian tapas restaurant Chuku's. I first asked her about her fondest memory of Plantain. She says: 'so, I thought about this and I can't think of my first memory of Plantain but that's primarily because I've got a bad memory. But when you asked me that question what actually happened was vignettes. Like coming to the kitchen as a child and seeing my mum fry Plantain and knowing it was going to be a good day.'

When I ask her about what Plantain culture means to her she goes on to explain: 'the first things I thought of were joy and love. It's interesting because I think the evolution of Plantain culture feels like it hasn't been synonymous with the more obvious or more vocal presence of Black British culture. I grew up in a very particular area and maybe someone else didn't feel this way and for me growing up, Plantain was a dish I was always having to explain to people. At school, at college, in uni. Like, I went to uni in Cambridge and I remember a group of us discovering where we could find it and it was like £1 for 1. It was mad.'

When I raise the topic of Plantain gentrification, the res-taurateur has an interesting outlook that is coloured by her experience in the restaurant industry.

'From the chef point of view, use of the ingredient isn't the issue. Gentrification of food is a separate issue, the issue is how does that restaurant play into the wider food culture and its relationship with the community that food comes from or exists in. I think there's conflation with wider problems and certain actions. Not every action is good or bad, the action itself is fairly neutral. I don't think fine dining restaurants using Plantain change the conversation around gentrification of food. Because then are you saying that a Nigerian fine dining restaurant shouldn't use Plantain? Or fine dining Latin American restaurants? Plantain belongs to so many cultures, globally, if those cultures start to emerge in the fine dining or food industry then Plantain should exist there too. I don't think things are as black and white as that. But the gentrification of food is another issue.'

IFEYINWA'S ABSOLUTE NO-GO:

'Chocolate. I have a personal beef with chocolate. I think it's a bit overrated. My thing is, Plantain is great and if you start mixing with chocolate, people are going to get gassed because it's chocolate and not Plantain, and Plantain will play second fiddle to this other ingredient. If you're playing with Plantain, it should be something that enhances it. I don't want to hear "Chocolate and Plantain." Plantain first. I'm sure you could create something nice, but people go too googly-eyed for chocolate. I'm not here for that.'

Dee Woods, an award-winning cook, food educator and researcher with over 20 years' experience of working in diverse communities had some thoughts to share too.

Dee's passion for the fruit is unrivalled. Not long into our conversation Dee explains her relationship with Plantain.

'Everyone knows my love for Plantain. I love joy and Plantain. It is one of those foods that I really really really love and somehow people don't get the politics behind it. And about where it comes from and who grows it and what does the farmer get, what are their conditions, what is happening to the biodiversity and I think for a lot of people all they care about is the price. If that changes tomorrow, where will it be? I'm the sort of person that's like "don't wait for tomorrow", what are we doing to ensure that we support our communities elsewhere and also to ensure that we're getting the best as well?'

Dee reflects on London in the 80s when Plantain was established within minority communities in the country, particularly Black British communities. She recounts being able to get the fruit in areas like Brixton and Shepherd's Bush Market. When asked about what community brought the fruit into the UK back in the 80's she says: 'It was mainly Caribbean people but then a lot of Asian people as well. Plantain, which originates from the Pacific, has come right through. We think of it as a Black food but it isn't. So many Polynesian friends eat Plantain. Asian people eat Plantain. South American people eat Plantain. And there's this big love for Plantain in all these different parts of the world.'

Dee, who, as you can tell, is like a walking Plantain encyclopedia, explains what Plantain means to her.

'Plantain culture is just appreciating it as a food. It derives great joy and comfort and it can be used from its green stage right through to its blackest. My son almost threw a black Plantain away and I said, "Noooo!" Different stages. Different things; he's used to seeing me use it green. My parents used to use it with sugar as well. You can make fufu, in so many different ways. You can even bake it. It's one of those foods you can use in so many different ways, savoury, sweet, etc.'

We speak about the potential direction Plantain might be taken in and I quiz Dee on her thoughts on Plantain possibly becoming a gourmet ingredient.

'I'm one of those people who's kicking up against, you know, this European thing about fine dining. There's something about home cooking, the value it holds within our families and our communities. We don't have to try and compete with this eurocentric view of fine dining.'

When it comes to the versatility of Plantain, Dee highlights some interesting historic uses of the fruit too.

'It was burned to make ash that produces soap. Black soap is used within Orisha culture for cleansing. So much we get from Plantain worldwide.'

Dee also swears by a certain ingredient being the perfect Plantain companion.

'Ooooo Plantain and chocolate! You have to try it. Not rubbish chocolate though. Has to be pure cacao and you have to have chilli in it. If you haven't had that, you haven't lived.'

DEE'S ABSOLUTE NO-GO:

'Brussel Sprouts? But you know what. I could even make that work.'

Another Plantain Republic member, Riaz Phillips is a writer and all-round creative raised in London. He is also the author of the book *Belly Full: Caribbean Food in the UK* and curator of the book *Community Comfort*. Riaz is also, of course, a Plantain lover. On the question of how to pronounce the word—Plan-tin or Plan-tain? Riaz answers saying, '[It depends on] the person I'm trying to sweeten up to give me a bigger portion. Whatever they say, I'm saying.' A smart answer indeed.

On his first memory of Plantain, Riaz answers simply: 'I don't really have a first memory. To me that's like asking what your early memories of milk or water are. It has always just been a part of life.' Riaz muses on how he never really learnt how to make Plantain, instead he simply picked it up by observing it being made so many times.

The London-based author reflects on the flexibility of the fruit and when asked about his thoughts when he thinks of Plantain, he says, 'complexity. It's amazing how differently it's cooked in different regions, be it Plan-tin, Plantain or Plátanos and then when you see all the additional ways it can be cooked i.e. fried, boiled, baked and then seasoned, served with other things. It just goes on and on.'

We have explored the importance of food within communities, and on this talking point, Riaz states, 'when a community is displaced or moves en masse to a new region, one of the initial outward facing displays it has in its new home are food and drink institutions.' He expands on this: 'when people want to connect or learn about a new community or their own heritage, apart from music, food is the next main element people turn to. This is why food and the spaces it creates are so pivotal.' Riaz Phillip's most recent book *Community Comfort* is a cookbook with recipes from more than 100 cooks and food enthusiasts with migrant backgrounds. Riaz tells me he didn't dictate what recipes people gave to the book but asserts, 'the diversity of foods using Plantain in there is incredible. There are Plantain curries, a number of vividly different snacks, a Plantain breakfast porridge, a Plantain dessert with ice cream and more, all inspired by heritages from across the world.'

When asked, 'what should one never ever ever do with Plantain when cooking, Riaz's response is, 'DON'T burn it!' Another piece of sound advice from Riaz is, 'support your local aunty/uncle grocery shop and stop complaining about their Plantain prices.'

Finally, Yvone Maxwell. A documentary photographer based in London going by the name *passthedutchpot*, a self-confessed Plantain lover and cooking enthusiast, whose first piece of published writing on the global food newsletter *Vittles* was of course, about Plantain.

I ask her about how she got into Plantain and she begins to explain: 'So in my day job I'm an IT consultant, but my creative outlet is photography, specifically documentary photography and portraiture. And Plantain has always been a love of mine. I was raised by a St Lucian mum, and I'm also half Nigerian. And literally, we had Plantain in my house every day. It was always in abundance. It was something that I grew up with. It was Saturday morning breakfast, you know, Plantain with some scrambled eggs. Mixing it up with some grilled tomatoes, doing all sorts of things. It was always a feature, roast dinners, Christmas dinners, everything.'

She goes on to explain how food and specifically Plantain became a focal point in her creative endeavours. 'As I kind of stepped into my photography, food became a focus of discussion and, I guess, kind of just the way my brain works, like I always gravitate towards food.'

Yvone shares with me her fondest Plantain memory: 'It was when I discovered that you can push Plantain outside of the molds that we know it. Especially within Blackness, right? Especially within African-Caribbean cuisine where you chop it, fry it, you know these things.'

Yvone's curiosity leads her to a serendipitous discovery. 'It's when I started exploring [Plantain] and messing with it. So I was watching MasterChef. And they had a dish called fondant potatoes. And I was like, I mean, could you not do this to Plantain? I mean... Because fondant potatoes are caramelized and so soft and fluffy in the middle. And I was like, What? This would bang as Plantain, like c'mon. So that weekend I attempted it. It was f@! amazing.'

Yvone's appreciation for Plantain is infectious. Her outlook on Plantain is expansive and she sees the fruit as limitless in terms of what can be done with it. She explains her joy at learning how the different cutting methods impact its flavor.

'I love the creative ways that it's cut... How that impacts the sweetness, and how that encourages caramelization... So obviously, if it's cut smaller, you get little mini hints of it. And also there's loads more of them, you know, as opposed to when it's sliced diagonally. I can usually tell when it's a Caribbean person serving me food by the way that the Plantain's been sliced. As opposed to a Nigerian. So I think that's also like an amazing discovery.'

Yvone shares her thoughts on the relationship Black people have with food. 'I think we have kind of internalized that the West is best, you know. If I hear another chef, or another cook, say, "trying to put African food or Caribbean food on the map," I'm gonna slap them. I'm tired of it. It's on the map. That's why jerk is a spice that you can find anywhere. That's why Jamie Oliver made jollof rice. It's a commercialized version that's on the map, that's what's on the map. Now let's dig a bit deeper. To me, I feel like we don't accept our food until it's been accepted by the West or by whiteness if you'd like.'

I will end this chapter with a statement Yvone made in our chat. It is a statement that sums up the sentiment of not just this book but also my relationship with Plantain.

'BUT YEAH, IN SHORT, PLANTAIN, THAT'S LIFE. BASICALLY.'

**PLANTAIN
WORD
COUNT:
390**

4

THE WAR OF PRONOUNCIATION: PLAN-TAIN VS. PLAN-TIN

Cool. So now that we're here. It's time to have the inevitable discussion that no book about Plantain can avoid. I know it's what some of you have been waiting for. This chapter is dedicated to the on-going linguistic war that has long divided Black British communities, for generations. To mark this moment, it's only right that I do my best literary Bruce Buffer attempt to mark the occasion.

Bruce Buffer Voice

Ahem. So, Ladies and gentlemen, galdem and mandem, children of God and otherwise, the moment you have all been waiting for. A bout for the ages. The debate of all debates. Brought to you by the world's most amazing, oil-frying, oven-roasting, fibre-packing sensation. A dialogue seeped deep into Black British diasporic culture. Inspired by 100% passion and maybe 1.7% facts. A debate as profound as the 'chicken or the egg'. Where words like mountain and fountain hold more phonetic weight than ever before. One side sporting straight jeans and suede clark wallabees, the other side boasting a range of agbadas and dashikis. One side heel-toeing as they dodge oil pops, the other doing the shaku as they duck the same thing.

The possible chink in the armour of Stefflon Don and Burna Boy's relationship. The only culinary query that matters.

Is it pronounced Plan-tain or Plan-tin?

Now maybe you already know the answer. Or better yet, you believe you do. You probably feel a sense of pride and prerogative when Plan-tin or Plan-tain rolls off your tongue. You may feel special jurisdiction over this topic owed to you by which side of the world you originate from. Either way, you are probably gagging to see if you were right all along. Query no more for everything will be cleared up. This discussion meets its conclusion here. A tall order I know, but in the end, it'll all make sense.

For those of you who understand the weight of this discussion, you have probably gathered your arguments, op-eds, peer reviews, statistical and qualitative data. For those of you who have read thus far and have no idea what I am talking about, stay tuned for the exploration of one of the most divisive conversations within the Black British community. A perennial war of words between Africans and Caribbeans nationwide. Let me explain.

Plantain, as expressed throughout this book, is a food at the centre of many Black and Brown cultures. When we look at Plantain within Black Britain and specifically within African and Caribbean communities, which much of this book does, we have learned Plantain is a culinary staple for both communities. Although African and Caribbean cuisine, ranging from Angola, Ghana, Nigeria, Ivory Coast and more, to Jamaica, Trinidad and Tobago, Dominican Republic, Haiti, Puerto Rico, etc. have stylistic differences, they share a lof things in common. Plantain is one of those things.

So when it comes to how Plantain is pronounced, they're both equally as invested. While my Anglophone-Carribean brethren pronounce the fruit 'Plan-Tin', my fellow

Anglo-phone primarily West Africans pronounce it 'Plan-Tain'.

Anglophone-Carribeans assert their pronunciation is correct for reasons that include, assessing how words that are spelt similarly to Plantain are pronounced. Namely words like 'fountain' and 'mountain'. The argument being that if 'mountain' is pronounced *moun-tin* then there is no rational reason that Plantain should be any different.

Anglophone West Africans' way of saying Plantain differs; they are adopters of the Plan-tain pronunciation. This argument relies on assessing the pronunciation of words like 'contain' and 'maintain' to Plantain. The view goes that if 'contain' is pronounced *con-tain* then so should Plantain.

Now what some of you might be asking, is it really that deep? What does it matter? Who cares? Tomato, tomata? Potato, potata? But what's at stake is so much more than you might think. Why? Because the winning side gets to yield ultimate bragging rights like you've never seen before. A chance to look to the other side and either say a densely stewed, 'See your life' or a well seasoned '*kmt** eediat' with absolute authority. It is very easy for this to come across as a feigned drama with no substantial context. A melodramatic saga between two groups of people who converge where Plantain is consumed anyway. But to see this as merely a silly cultural dispute not only undermines the cultural significance of Plantain in Afro-Caribbean communities and culture, but it also overlooks how important accurate etymology of foods is in general. Renaming is often the first strike in the battle against 'food gentrification' where the gentrifier attempts to re-discover a food by renouncing the historical, cultural and even trade relationship Black and Brown communities have with it.

The Plan-tin vs Plan-tain ting isn't just an unimportant

---

* Kiss my teeth—a sound made by kissing one's teeth to show disrespect or disapproval .

bickering session between Black folks on the Twitter timeline. It is a critical debate delineative of the cultural significance of Plantain within the Black diasporic community in the UK. It usually happens orally without any archived, recorded or conclusive data left to be regurgitated in the next barbeque or party. So, my editor thought what better way to tackle this than to produce some statistical data that finally puts some numbers to it. After all, the saying goes, men lie, women lie, but numbers don't lie. Of course these numbers won't serve as any proof of grammatical authority, but they will at least give one side of the argument some well-deserved clout.

So, we put together the British Plantain survey and we had over 400 participants. The survey results were interesting, funny and in some ways insightful. The singular thing that came across was the level of ownership participants felt over Plantain and its name. What can I say? People really love Plantain!

Sixty-three point two per cent of the participants were aged between 25–34, 16.9% were between the ages 18–24, 12.9% were aged between 35–44 and 3% were aged between 55–64. So it's safe to say, the participants were a young bunch. Yes, 25–34 year olds, you're still young.

Thrity-one point seven per cent of the participants admitted to consuming Plantain 'at least once a month', 24.6% said they consumed the delicacy 'at least once a week' and 24.6% of participants agreed to eating the fruit every couple of days (my kind of people).

Overwhelmingly, our participants were either from Nigeria, Ghana or Jamaica, which one would expect. We also had a noticeable amount of people from Sierra Leona, Barbados, Uganda, Angola and Zimbabwe.

An overwhelming majority stated they noticed an increase in the price of Plantain in the last 5–10 years, 79% of participants to be exact.

In the section of the survey where participants were asked to explain why they chose their selected pronunciation of Plantain, there were expected responses like, 'because it's correct!' and, 'that is just the way it is'. There were also many answers that were rooted in attempts at linguistic prowess, namely that Plantain is similar to words like 'mountain' and 'fountain' and thus it should be pronounced 'Plan-TIN' or the argument that many West Africans in the survey made, which was that Plantain is similar to words like 'sustain' or 'contain' and thus should be pronounced 'Plant-TAIN'. However, the most frequent response from participants was their admission that they chose their pronunciation based on how their parents pronounced the fruit's name or how people from their country pronounced it.

Without further ado though, we can reveal the numbers behind the most important question of our time. Before the reveal, I would like to thank every Plantain loving human being who took the time to take part in the survey. This one's for you.

DRUM ROLL PLEASE… By a very slim margin, the winner, at least according to this Plantain survey is ……. PLAN-TAIN!!

Yes, that's right. 55.4% of participants chose 'Plan-tain' as the correct pronunciation of the fruit and 40.6% chose 'Plan-tin'

as the correct pronunciation. What does this show us? That Africans can never hold last. Of course, this survey does not settle the dispute. We will actually get to the bottom of that shortly. But, it does provide some data on just how passionately all the participants feel about the fruit and how the societal and cultural exploration of the fruit is validated by its consumers.

As I reflect on the results of the survey, for me, the different pronunciations of Plantain are nothing more than evidence of how much we love the fruit. If there was no love, we wouldn't care enough to pronounce it in our own ways let alone debate over it.

It takes me back to my conversation with photographer Yvone Maxwell. There was a point in our chat where Yvone began telling me about an article she wrote on Plantain and the Black community's fixation with its pronunciation. She went on to explain why she felt it was not necessarily a useful debate to have: 'If someone from Colombia came to you and said, do you want some Plátanos? You're not going to correct them. You're not gonna go, "actually, it's Plantin or Plantain". And I think we forget that within Blackness, there are different facets of Blackness, right? There are different pronunciations of things, there are different ways of cooking stuff. And I think with Plantain, it's literally just a distraction. Like, it's just a pronunciation.'

She expands more: 'I think because we're all Black, we expect there to be one way of doing this. There's one way of saying this, and there's one way of cooking this, when actually there are so many ways, even within our Blackness, that we celebrate and utilize and maximize Plantain.'

In total agreement, the important thing is that Plantain is ours. But of course, that simply won't do. Somebody needs to win. And so, we move.

A large part of this battle hinges on one particular rule from the English language that inspires an argument that we've heard many times.

'So hOw dO yoU sAy moUntAiN?'

This argument put across by Anglophone Caribbeans, seemingly puts, they think, the Plan-TAIN pronunciation to bed. But how many of you really understand it though? And does it really hold as much weight as we think it does? The argument is that the word 'Plantain', being a noun, mirrors the phonetic implication of other nouns with the suffix 'ain'. Words like 'mountain', 'fountain' that results in a 'tin' pronunciation. Whereas verbs with the suffix 'ain' like 'contain' or 'maintain' have the 'tain' pronunciation. Sounds good, but let's explore this further.

The argument insists that Plantain should be pronounced the same way as words like 'mountain' and 'fountain' because of supposed effects of nouns on pronunciation. Is there any truth to this? Slightly. This argument hinges on the concept of stress and vowel reduction in English, specifically that of syllabic stresses. Stay with me.

There are a number of rules and things to note when it comes to syllabic stresses. The most important ones being what we call primary stress, secondary stress and unstressed syllables. These stresses tell you how to pronounce a word. Usually the primary stress is the syllable of a word that is said longer, louder, clearer and with a particular pitch on the vowel. This in turn can completely change the pronunciation of said word. The secondary stress is the syllable that is weaker than the primary stress. For example, 'crazy' has two syllables /CRAY-zee/, and the 'cray' is the primary stress while the latter 'zee' is the secondary. Which is why you might hear someone say 'that's cray cray' but never 'that's zee zee'.

Unstressed syllables are syllables with no stress at all. An example being the word 'prepare' that has two syllables /pruh-PAIR/ and the 'pre' is commonly rushed through. Hence being the unstressed syllable while 'pair' is the primary stressed syllable.

In words like 'mountain' and 'contain' and of course 'Plantain', there are two syllables.

/MOUN-tn/

/kun-TEYN/

And for Plantain it will either be

/PLANT-tn/ where the primary stress in on the first syllable whether you say 'a' or 'ah'

Or

/plan-TEYN/ where the primary stress is on the second syllable. Again, whether you say 'a' or 'ah' is more a choice than by instruction.

The general rule is that when the word is a noun, the stress is usually placed on the first syllable. Whereas with a verb, the stress is on the second syllable and as a rule, the first syllable must be unstressed. So, in words like 'contain' or 'sustain' the stress is on the 'tain' and the first part of the word is unstressed.

The rule becomes even more apparent when we find words

with the same spelling but different pronunciation. Known as heterophones, these are words like 'produce' and 'address' which depending on whether they are said as nouns or verbs require different placements of syllabic stresses.

Examples:

Address when used as a noun:
/AD-dress/

As a verb:
/ad-DRESS/

Produce when used as a noun:
/PRO-duce/

As a verb:
/pro-DUCE/

Project when used as a noun:
/PROJ-ect/

As a verb:
/pro-JECT/

Contract when used as a noun:
/CON-tract/

As a verb:
/con-TRACT/

And so on. The trend we start to see is that the verbs have their primary stresses on the second syllable and the nouns have theirs on the first.

So what does this all mean, Plantain? Well for all my fellow West Africans it is a devastating blow. When I was writing this, I almost wanted to believe it wasn't true.

According to this rule, Plantain is a noun and thus we would apply the primary stress on the first syllable similar to 'mountain'. So in effect the 'plan' gets stressed to sound like the word 'plan' or 'plant' and the second part of the word would naturally be unstressed.

Which means, according to the English language, the following pronunciation would be used.

/PLAN-tn/ also spelt, Plan-tin

Yes. The Caribbeans win. I DON'T MAKE THE RULES.

So boom. Query finished? The rules are the rules. Pack back your bags and go home. What else is there to be said?

Well, no. Not exactly.

Why? Because bun the English language. In most regards the placement of stresses is highly dependent on who is speaking. The reality is that there are many English words that are pronounced differently by American, English and African people, and there is no real reason for this. The difference is simply due to differing accents and cultures.

Why should Africans or Caribbeans undermine their pronunciations of Plantain to appease a set of linguistic rules from people who don't even know Plantain?

In an article the BBC posted, 'Does your accent make you sound smarter?' Chi Luu, a resident linguist at *JSTOR*, wrote, 'a standard dialect is simply one local variety of a language which has become most publicly accepted in social institutions.' What social institutions are we waiting to induct our Plantain pronunciations in? Surely none. So long as we enjoy this fruit, none of this even matters.

In an article by the conversation entitled, 'Why Does the UK Have So Many Accents?'; Natalie Barber, a professor of linguistics at Nottingham Trent Uni, wrote: 'Where we come from matters. Our origins form an important part of a distinctive personality, which can become a group identity when we share these origins. More often than not, our use of language, especially our dialect, is an expression of that distinctiveness.'

PLANTAIN WORD COUNT: 431

I don't think it's worth undermining the distinctiveness of our Plantain communities for small small babylonian English. Whether you're part of the Plan-tin crew or the Plan-tain crew. Jos enjoy your ting. We all win.

5

PLANTAIN ALL OVER THE WORLD

Earlier, I said I'd be writing in a Black British context. The importance of this is obvious. With regards to Plantain in Britain, it's Black British diasporas alone that amplify its significance. It's our communities who give life to the long-standing lingual warfare that is Plan-tain vs Plan-tin. It is the Black British diaspora that creates safe online spaces to discuss the beauty of the fruit. From Plantain-themed apparel, magazines, neologisms—it all comes from the Plantain loving Black community. We have assumed a *de facto* ownership of the fruit that knows no boundaries. We claim Plantain wholeheartedly with both our hands and refuse to give it up.

However, our inexorable dominion over Plantain does produce an oversight. As much as we know and love Plantain, our protectiveness has, in some ways, prevented us from seeing just how culturally expansive this fruit really is. That's to say: our greatest feat in keeping Plantain 'Black' is also where we find fault. Sounds dramatic, I know. And it's also not to say the grass is, by comparison, greener on the other side. I don't know what Marco Pierre White would do with a ripe Plantain in his hand. After the culinary travesty that saw him make what can only be described as neo-colonialism on a plate, aka his shocking attempt at what he called 'Jamaican Rice and Peas.' I have no interest to see what he would do with Plantain.

We do extraordinary things with Plantain, from turning Black Plantain that people might throw away into Kelewele or beautifully oven-baked Jamaican Patties and much more. But as Yvonne Maxwell explained: 'The greatest superpower of Plantain is its versatility'. Evidenced by how many different cultures have adapted it to their palates and cuisines... Plantain offers a world of possibilities that is as diverse as the cultures that consume it. So, in this chapter we will expand our lens to the global world of Plantain eaters and explore how Plantain is eaten and loved in other parts of the world. I should state that I, of course, couldn't cover every single way, recipe and remix of Plantain dishes but I have picked ones I think that you will enjoy reading about and particularly took my interest.

In all its single glory, Plantain is far from a monolith. And I don't just mean that in a poetic way. When I say that Plantain is not a monolith, I mean it in a very literal sense. Yes, Plantain is Plantain. But the kind of Plantain used in Minatamis Na Saging, a Filipino delicacy, eaten as a dessert, is not the same as the Plantain used in your daily dose of Dodo (Yoruba for fried Plantain). Remember, there are over 100 Plantain and banana cultivars, each subtle in their distinction but distinct nonetheless.

All of this information may seem trivial at first. Afterall, most of us aren't agriculturalists and most of us only know and care for three different types of Plantain: green, yellow and black. But the importance of knowing the different varieties of what we consider the 'cooking banana' surfaces when we look at what some people call the Ugandan Plantain, AKA the Matoke. Treasured as a staple food in Uganda. Matoke looks and feels like Green Plantain, albeit the kid version. It peels like a very stubborn Green Plantain, boils like Green Plantain and tastes like Green Plantain. However, despite its high starch content, thick skin and biological properties that are practically interchangeable with Plantain, the East African Highland Banana, which is the name for the Matoke cultivar, is, botanically speaking, not a Plantain at all. In fact, it shares the same genome group, AAA, with the more widely known Cavendish banana. The soft, easily peelable and eaten raw banana. And while there are some Ugandans who might care to distinguish Matoke from Plantain and will state such in their online recipes, there are others who choose not to.

Similar questions arise when looking across countries like Malaysia and Myanmar, where the divergence of banana cultivars and varieties are so great in numbers, people don't bother with any distinctions.

Search for an Indonesian Pisang Goreng online and you might find people saying it's a banana fritter and others saying it's a Plantain fritter. And even though it's traditionally made with Plantain, it can be made interchangeably with banana. In the Philippines, the Saba looks and cooks exactly like what you'd imagine a baby Plantain might look and cook like. And even though it's popularised as such, it's not actually Plantain. We can even go to the Pacific Islands, where the Fe'i, a Polynesian banana, not to be confused with the Red Banana, gets called the 'mountain Plantain' due to its high starch content and bright red, orangey skin that is roasted and boiled like the Plantain you know. Yet it belongs in its own Musa category, so it's definitely not a 'true Plantain'.

With all the obscurities in the Musa family, it gets hard to keep track of what's what, especially when looking at Plantains. Before I knew the details of banana genetics, when I first looked at someone peeling, slicing and deep-frying Matoke, I wouldn't have thought twice about calling it a Green Plantain. Same goes for other aforementioned banana cultivars that share their genome group with 'dessert bananas'; Cavendish bananas, red bananas, Gros Michel, etc. but get cooked and consumed like bootleg Plantains. So what then does that mean for the Plantain vs Banana dichotomy that we're so ready to chop someone's head off for? How does it shape our knowledge and understanding of Plantain?

In answering this question, a little bit of intellectual dishonesty has to be applied. A quality of dishonesty that acknowledges the biological distinctions between true bananas and true Plantains but is ready to dismiss it all, at the expense of upholding the cherished Plantain vs Banana dichotomy that we've adhered to. We can't just let it go because of one or two discrepancies. The true value of the Plantain vs Banana dichotomy is in the difference of how the two are cooked and eaten. The peeling, the roasting, the boiling, the slicing, the frying. If Cavendish bananas cooked like Plantain did, no one would care to distinguish the two. But part of what makes Plantain so special, aside from the incredible taste, is the labour of love you put into it. From the careful and poised yet intuitive way you run your knife over the lines in the skin to knowing the correct ripeness. Plantain is a whole process. And so for the banana cultivars that aren't exactly Plantains but require the same labour of love and possess the durability to stand firm in a sea full of scorching, bubbling oil and not break like their lesser genome counterparts, we will acknowledge them as 'faux-Plantains'. In order to enjoy everything that Plantain culture around the world has to offer. Furthermore, some of these cultivars are cooked as a matter of custom rather than necessity. Meaning that they can actually be eaten raw, as their starch content converts to sugars when they ripen but instead are appreciated for their clandestine Plantain identity, fried, boiled, roasted and baked for true enjoyment.

This isn't to say that you can just grab any common banana, slap it in a fryer and call it Plantain. The prerequisites for qualifying as a faux-Plantain (that's what I'm calling them from now on) is that: it has the durability to swim in bubbling hell-fire oil and come out with new refined aesthetic, is overflowing with starch content and, true to the variety of Plantain, has at least five ways to be wonderfully cooked.

From Puerto Rico all the way in North America, to the Philippines all the way in South East Asia, there are Plantain loving communities all over the world. The experience researching this has been pleasantly enlightening, presenting me with new and creative ways to look at Plantain. And for Plantain lovers like me, you're either going to be equally as impressed or disturbed.[*]

AFRICA

So we will start with the motherland. The source. The source with the sauce. The land that collectively produces more Plantain than the rest of the globe combined.[1] The land that in 2018 was responsible for 59% of the total consumption of Plantain in the world.[2] That's a lot of Dodo and Kakro. It is, of course, Africa.

In West Africa, Plantains, along with bananas, are mostly planted at the onset of the rainy season, along with other crops like rice, cassava and maize. With the major harvest between the months of November and February, Plantain grows when most other starchy crops are unavailable or difficult to harvest. Therefore, Plantain plays a key role in the provision of food security throughout the region. Particularly when facing food scarcity in the dry season.[3]

The love of Plantain in Africa is wired deep into its cuisine and has shaped some of the most quintessential African dishes and snacks throughout the times. So much so that Plantain

---

[*] All recipes should be read with the reader's discretion and can be tweaked to your flavour. Enjoy!

traditions have been carried through the diasporas. From the Netherlands, to Portugal, to France and of course the United Kingdom where love for Plantain permeates throughout Black British homes and in some of our high streets.

Heading first over to East Africa. Supposedly where the very first bunches of Plantain brought to the region were found.

We start with Uganda, referred to by some as the Banana Republic of Africa, sometimes interchangeably with Kenya and Tanzania. Here we see both the aforementioned faux-Plantains and true Plantain cultivars are renowned as jewels of Ugandan cuisine. Staple food for families across the country all year round. The 'true Plantains' (AAB) make up less of the 50+ varieties of banana cultivars produced in the country. Still, 'Gonja', not to be confused with the kingdom in Ghana, the name attributed to Plantain cultivars, are still enjoyed with infectious zest across the land. In fact, seeing Gonja donuts was the first time I had even thought about the concept of Plantain ringed donuts. When I first saw them on Sophie Musoki's page, a Ugandan food blogger and writer, my mind went *boom*.

Still, no 'true Plantain' cultivar is as heavily consumed in Uganda as the East African Highland Banana, more commonly known as Matoke. Fitting into our faux-Plantain category, Matoke is probably the most popular cultivar produced in Uganda. Consumed mostly in its ripe form, Matoke can easily be mistaken for a green Plantain. It's just as tough to peel and it boils and fries in a similar way. It's so heavily ingrained into the culture of Ugandan cuisine that Matoke has long been recognized as Uganda's national dish. And even though Matoke can be cooked in a number of ways, it is common to see it cooked in a stew, either boiled or boiled and mashed. The dish is primarily a Matoke-based stew and can be made with beef, as it often is, or with a vegan twist, which is also just as popular. Now when looking at online recipes, it can be very easy for *some* to mistake the large chops of Matoke found in stew and mistake it for potatoes.

Matoke recipes are also enjoyed across Kenya. The way in which the two countries use Matoke, and 'true Plantains' for that matter, are in some ways interchangeable.

For the recipe we're looking at, I managed to get a hold of Sophia Musoki of *A Kitchen in Uganda*, who penned a recipe for 'Katogo', a classic Matoke recipe. There are also recipes for using 'true Plantains' that you can find at Sophia's *A Kitchen in Uganda* page, along with other amazing recipes sure to sweet your palate.

CLASSIC KATOGO

INGREDIENTS	AUTHOR'S COMMENTS
15-20 Green Bananas (Matoke)	Applying oil to your hands before peeling the bananas prevents the sap from staining and sticking to your hands.
10 Medium Sized Tomatoes	
1 Large Onion	The amount of water you add to the katogo will determine the consistency of your katogo. More water will make it soupy and vice versa.
2 Scallion Stalks	
1 Tsp. Oil + Additional 1/2 Tsp. Oil	Sometimes a lot of tomatoes can make the food a little bit tart. If so, add a little bit of sugar to cut through the tartness.
Salt and Pepper	

METHOD

1. Apply the 1/2 teaspoon of oil on your hands and the knife you will be using and peel the matoke.
2. Place the peeled matoke in water to avoid excessive oxidation then dice the tomatoes and onions (and scallions) and set aside.
3. Place a clean pan on fire and add the teaspoon of oil. Add the onions and let them cook till translucent.
4. Next add the tomatoes and let them cook till tender and paste-like this will be your stew base for the Katogo).

Credit: A Kitchen in Uganda

Not yet departing from East Africa, we have a look at another East African country that very seldom gets associated with Plantain. But even in a country like Somalia where Plantain isn't woven into the fabric of their culinary DNA, Plantain is out there doing God's work. Literally. During Ramadan, after long days of fasting, Muslims all around the world rejoice in the bounty of Allah with a well-deserved Iftar. Consisting of a few plump dates per person and a myriad of halal delicacies. And it is within this myriad of delicacies that we can sometimes find Moos Bukeni, sometimes spelt 'Moos Bukeeni', a sweetened dessert made up of ripe Plantains. Moos Bukeni is a Somali dish traditionally eaten as a dessert, cooked quite similar to Bataato Macaan, a Somali dish that utilizes sweet potato. Layering it with a syrup-like texture but obviously less sumptuous because it isn't Plantain. Moos Bukeni can be made with whatever variety of Plantain shapes and slices of your choosing and although the dish is usually made with coconut milk, water can also be used.

MOOS BUKENI

INGREDIENTS	AUTHOR'S COMMENTS
5 Plantains (Ripe)	One way of making this dish is using coconut milk, however my parents cannot eat food with coconut milk so this recipe is just for making the Plantain using sugar syrup. This is similar to Bataato Macaan. You can make it with coconut milk or just water.
1 Cup Granulated Sugar	
½ Tsp Cardamom Powder	
2 Tbsp Ghee	
Water	

PREP TIME: 5 MINUTES
COOK TIME: 10 MINUTES
TOTAL TIME: 15 MINUTES

METHOD

1. Peel the Plantains, cut them into thin pieces.
2. In a pan, pour ¼ of the sugar and let this brown completely. Keep stirring so the sugar doesn't burn.
3. Once the sugar is dark, add the Plantains, water (1 cup).
4. Cover the pan and let the Plantains cook until they are soft and the sugar syrup has thickened.

Credit: Sikia Cooking

Moving on then to the West of Africa, my home away from home. All over West Africa, Plantain is enjoyed as a customary, yet extraordinary, facet of the West African diet. Whether it's a young green Plantain, a slightly grown and blemished yellow Plantain or a blacker the skin, sweeter the starch, black Plantain.

In Nigeria, Plantain is a huge staple food. So much so, that in 2020, in Osun State, a 35 year-old man, obviously hit with a strong case of Plantain withdrawal, risked one month of his freedom for roughly £100 worth of Plantain after being caught trying to steal it. They can lock the locks, but they can't stop the clocks. Free my guy. [4]

In Nigeria, Plantain is often enjoyed on its own or along with bright orange parboiled Jollof rice. Of course, the long-grain variety. You can also find the ripest of Plantain, even that which some may think is unusable, either too dark, or too soft, used in recipes like Dodo Ikire. Where overripe Plantain is mashed, often with mixed 'peppeh', and deep fried in hot palm oil. I have included the exact recipe from *MyActiveKitchen* on the next page, a website dedicated to home-cooked food by Ajoke, a food blogger, photographer and spice maker based in Manchester.

You'd think that the ubiquity of Dodo speaks to or may indicate a one-dimensional approach Nigerians have to cooking Plantain. But you couldn't be more wrong. Cooked often in a similar fashion to Mexican tamales, Nigerians have a dish called Moimoi, or 'Moin-moin' as it's also called. Cooked usually with Thaumatococcus Daniellii, or what Yorubas call Ewe Eran leaves. Akwukwo Elele by Igbos. Moin-moin is best described as a savoury steamed bean pudding. Blended with a mixture of beans, peppers, onions and different spices. However, it can also be made with Plantain, trading names between Epiti and Ukpo Ogede.

DODO IKIRE

INGREDIENTS	AUTHOR'S COMMENTS
2-3 Overripe Plantains (Black or Yellow Turning Black) Salt to Taste Palm Oil Crushed Chilli (Use according to preference)	'Dodo Ikire' is one of the popular snacks a kid would ask his/her parents to buy when they are going on a journey to some parts of Nigeria, the south-west to be precise. Or should I speak for myself, I remember as a child anytime my parents were travelling outside Abeokuta, the first thing I'd say to them after wishing them a safe journey apparently was 'e ba mi ra dodo Ikire bo o' (buy some Dodo Ikire for me on your way back home). I also remember my mum making this for us amongst other Plantain snacks anytime we had overripe Plantain.

METHOD

1. Peel and finely chop or mash the Plantains.
2. Transfer the Plantains into a bowl, add in your salt, crushed chilli and mix together until they are well combined then set aside.
3. Place a frying pan on medium heat, add a decent amount of palm oil, enough to submerge each Plantain scoop half way, and then allow to heat for 3-4 minutes.
4. When hot, scoop portions of the Plantain mix into the oil with a spoon and cook until they brown on both sides (reduce the heat whilst frying so the Plantain cooks through and doesn't overcook/burn).
5. Remove from the heat and drain the Dodo Ikire on kitchen towels to absorb the excess oil.
6. When cool, use your hand to better shape each scoop and then put tightly in cling film.
7. Remove cling film after 4–5 minutes and serve.

Credit: MyActiveKitchen

UKPO OGEDE (NIGERIAN PLANTAIN PUDDING)

INGREDIENTS	AUTHOR'S COMMENTS
3 Overripe Plantains (Overripe/ Black)	It is quick and easy to make. Ukpo Ogede is soft, sweet and savoury all at the same time. Usually, Plantain flour or cornmeal is added to the overripe Plantain to give it more body or firmness and cut down the sweetness. You can also add unripe Plantain, it will taste good but the pudding will be a very deep brown colour. I haven't tried plain flour and polenta, but I hear they work well too. I will give them a try and let you know.
½ Medium Onions (¼ Chopped)	
2 ½ Tbsp Ground Crayfish	
1 Scotch Bonnet / Fresh pepper	
⅔ Cup of Cornmeal	
¼–½ Cup of Water	
Salt to Taste	
¼ Cup of Palm Oil	Ukpo Ogede needs the heat of chilli to balance the sweetness of the Plantain.

METHOD

1. Prepare small bowls by oiling them, make aluminum foil envelopes or wash banana leaves and set aside.
2. Wash, peel and cut Plantains into chunks.
3. Place Plantains, onion, crayfish, pepper, cornmeal and water in a blender: Grind until you get a smooth consistency.
4. Pour into a bowl, add salt and palm oil. Mix till well incorporated.
5. Taste for salt and adjust.
6. Pour into a prepared bowl, aluminium foil envelopes or wrap in banana leaves.
7. Steam for about 45 minutes. Then allow it to cool, becoming firm.
8. Eat on its own, with pap, rice or beans.

Credit: The Pretend Chef

In a similar fashion to how Plantain is valued in Nigeria, their basmati-cooking Jollof rivals also boast wholesome ways to harness Plantain goodness. Kakro is a Ghanaian dish that makes use of the black Plantain. Kakro, also pronounced Kaklo, meaning 'fried', is a dish you can find all over Ghana. It can be made both with regular ripe Plantain but is best reserved like its Nigerian counterpart, for sweet black Plantain. Traditionally, Kakro is made in an asanka, a Ghanian grinding pot.

KAKRO (KAKLO)

SERVINGS: 24 FRITTERS

INGREDIENTS	AUTHOR'S COMMENTS
4 Plantains (very ripe)	With fewer ingredients and less cooking time, the preparation of kakro is quite simple and straight-forward. The star ingredient of this dish is plantain and an important thing to consider while making kakro is to make use of an overripe plantain. Ripe plantains are soft and mushy and yellow in color like a banana.
1 Cup of All Purpose Flour	
1 Small Onion, Finely Grated	
1 Tbsp Chopped Fresh Ginger	
1 Tsp Salt	
1 Tsp Cayenne Pepper	
Vegetable Oil (for frying)	

With fewer ingredients and less cooking time, the preparation of kakro is quite simple and straight-forward. The star ingredient of this dish is plantain and an important thing to consider while making kakro is to make use of an overripe plantain. Ripe plantains are soft and mushy and yellow in color like a banana.

Hence leftover plantains that have become black in color are best to make kakro. If ripe plantains are not readily available in the markets, you can also ripen a green plantain by placing it in a brown paper bag. Depending on the climatic conditions of your region it might take a week or more to ripen.

Kaklo is enjoyed as a snack or as a light meal and is often accompanied by a stew or sauce. Krakro along with a spicy black-eyed bean stew, red red and palm oil, is a popular meal of the Ghanaian workers as it provides energy sustainable throughout the day. Sometimes, it is served as an appetizer or the locals also enjoy kakro as a street food

KAKRO (KAKLO) [CONT.]

PREP TIME: 15 MINUTES
COOK TIME: 15 MINUTES
TOTAL TIME: 30 MINUTES

METHOD

1. Peel the Plantains and place them in a bowl.
2. Mash them with a fork until obtaining a lumpy mixture.
3. Add the onion, ginger, salt, cayenne pepper and mix well with a spatula.
4. Add the flour and mix well.
5. In a deep skillet, heat a large volume of oil over medium heat.
6. Using a spoon, take some of the dough and dip in hot oil.
7. Fry on both sides until golden brown.
8. Place Kakro as you can a sheet of paper towels to remove excess oil.
9. Serve hot or warm.

Credit: 196flavors.com

Next, hailing from one of Africa's smallest nations, Togo, a candied Plantain treat called Ahayoe. A charming place with over 40 ethnic groups stretched across coastal plains, woodland plateaus, savannas, lagoons and marshes, how the Togolese popularised the closest thing to a Plantain take on a chocolate rice krispies cake is a lesson in gifted creativity. Sweet and savoury with its flavours, Ahayoe is simple in its process and spectacular in its outcome.

AHAYOE

SERVINGS: 3

INGREDIENTS	AUTHOR'S COMMENTS
2 Ripe Plantains	The mixture is fried till you either have a crunchy CoCo Pop type of texture or remove it immediately as it starts to brown for a softer version.
1 Medium Sized-Onion	
1 Litre of Oil	This recipe makes for a crunchy version and is a firm favourite of mine.
½ Teaspoon of Salt	This dish is also popular amongst the Ewes of Ghana and it's a must try.
	It's imperative to get rid of the excess oil by using a colander and transferring into a mould tin to shape it perfectly.

PREP TIME: 15 MINUTES
COOK TIME: 30 MINUTES
TOTAL TIME: 45 MINUTES

METHOD

1. Top and bottom the onion and slice into 2 equal parts.
2. Cut across the width of each Plantain into two equal parts.
3. Grate both Plantain and onion into a bowl. Once grated, add salt and mix well.
4. Place the mixture into a large frying pan with oil on medium/ high heat. Occasionally run through the mixture with a ladle or a similar utensil to cook evenly and avoid sticking.
5. Fry for 8-10 minutes.
6. Dry the Kakro on paper towels and place into chosen mould tin to shape.
7. Let cool and serve.

Credit: (Ndudu by Fafa)

Next on our list of African Plantain-loving nations is Equatorial Guinea. Located in what's considered Central Africa, Equatorial Guinea is known for being the only Spanish speaking country on the continent. The country is unique for many reasons and one of those is due to it being the origin of a brilliant breakfast dish called Akwadu. The dish can be cooked with either Cavendish bananas or Plantain but is more commonly associated with the latter and of course, is better enjoyed with Plantains.

AKWADU

SERVINGS: 4

INGREDIENTS

4 Plantains

1 Cup Shredded Coconut

½ Cup Orange Juice

¼ Cup Brown Sugar

3 Tbsp Melted Butter

2 Lemons, Squeezed

Honey to Taste

Cinamon to Taste (optional)

PREP TIME: 10 MINUTES
COOK TIME: 20 MINUTES
TOTAL TIME: 30 MINUTES

METHOD

1. Preheat your oven to 400°F.
2. Cut the Plantains in half lengthwise without removing the skin, along the top through to the bottom into two long parts each.
3. Score the Plantains a few times and place them in a baking dish.
4. Pour the butter over the Plantains, then drizzle the orange and lemon juices.
5. Sprinkle the sugar generously over the mix in the tray before adding the shredded coconut and cinnamon (optional).
6. Bake for 20 mins, basting regularly with the juices flowing into the dish.
7. Remove the bananas from the oven, drizzling honey on each slice.
8. Place in the oven grill and brown the top for a golden brown colour (for roughly 5 minute with close watching).
9. Serve when warm and enjoy.

Credit: 196flavors.com

Since we're out here baking: we go to a recipe taken from Liberian cuisine and take a look at Liberian Rice Bread. Yes, that's what it's called. Traditionally made with 'country' rice and overripe Plantain. It looks a bit like banana cake but made with rice beaten with a pestle in a mortar and slushy Plantain.

RICE BREAD

INGREDIENTS

2 Cups of Rice Flour

3 Mashed Plantains (Ripe or Overripe)

1 Cup Whole Milk (Or Alternatives)

2 Large Eggs

¼ Cup Granulated Sugar

½ Teaspoon Nutmeg

½ Teaspoon Ginger

½ Teaspoon Salt

1 Teaspoon Baking Soda

½ Cup Vegetable Oil

METHOD

1. Preheat the oven to 350 degrees.
2. In a large mixing bowl add all the ingredients and stir until they're thoroughly blended.
3. Bake in a well-greased loaf pan for about 40 minutes.

Credit: The African Gourmet

Eight hundred miles away, we take a peek through the curtain of a Malian kitchen. The dish I've chosen is Foutou Banane (Fufu de Plantain). This delicacy is also popular in the Ivory Coast and can be enjoyed with Aya Nakamura in the background giving strong Malian vibes. The Foutou Banane looks like what you'd imagine Plantain Fufu to look like. Soft, smooth, vibrantly yellow and ready to be submerged in thick stew. It is prepared in a similar fashion to Lituma, a mashed and boiled variety of Plantain from Congo or Ntouba Ekon another similar dish of a dryer consistency from Cameroon. The manner in which Foutou Banane is cooked can be found all over the continent.

FOUTOU BANANE

SERVINGS: 2

INGREDIENTS	AUTHOR'S COMMENTS
4 Ripe Plantains	Banana Foutou, also known as Banana Foufou in some African countries, is an excellent accompaniment to African sauces.
1 Cassava	
Salt to Taste	You can also add a little flour in the making to thicken up the balls.
2 Tbsp of Palm Oil	Personally I love the Foutou Banane where the recipe is made with ripe Plantains and fresh cassava.
Water	

TOTAL TIME: 30 MINUTES

METHOD

1. Peel the cassava and dice it then peel the Plantains and cut them into three pieces each.
2. In a pot, add the cassava and the Plantains and cover with salt and water. Boil until they are cooked through, which will be about 20-25 minutes.
3. Remove the cassava and Plantains from the water then use a mortar to pound the cassava until it becomes smooth. Add the Plantains little by little, continuing to pound the mixture until it becomes even smoother.
4. Add the palm oil and salt to the mixture and continue to pound.
5. Once cooled, use your hands to shape foutou balls out of the mixture.
6. Serve in a stew or sauce.

Credit: Recettes Africane

Next we look at a dish coming out of Cameroon, Plantain Porridge. Although there are Plantain Porridge dishes found in the Caribbean that look more like what you'd expect a dish called Plantain Porridge to look like. The Plantain Porridge I am referring to here is a dish with a West African twist, meaning it is palm-oil-based, Maggi-infused, meat-and-fish-filled delicacy. The dish, also known as Sese Plantain, has the Plantains tossed in a bowl with palm oil, a process known as 'sese'. Also called Born House Planti, 'born house' being

BORN HOUSE PLANTI/PLANTAIN PORRIDGE	
INGREDIENTS	AUTHOR'S COMMENTS
4-5 Unripe Plantains, Peeled and Cut in Halves	Avoid stirring the pot as much as you can while cooking. Hold both sides of the pot and shake to make the ingredients distribute evenly. If you must stir, do so with a wooden spoon.
½ Cup of Palm Oil	
1 Pound Smoked Fish and Meat of Choice	If you wish, add tomatoes to yours. I prefer mine without.
½ Cup Crayfish	
1 Maggi Crevette (Seasoning Cube) or 2 Teaspoons of Bouillon Powder	
2 Tbsp Blended Garlic and Ginger (optional)	
1 Habanero Pepper (optional)	
½ Country/Small Onion (Sliced)	
3-4 Handfuls Green Leafy Vegetable (I used Spinach while Bitterleaf is traditionally used)	

Cameroonian vernacular to describe 'a ceremony that is (or was) usually organised to welcome a new mother and her baby.'[5] And of course, to compliment the marvel of bringing new life into the world, the meal is traditionally and appropriately cooked with Plantain.

Again, Plantain's cultural significance knows no bounds.

BORN HOUSE PLANTI/PLANTAIN PORRIDGE

PREP TIME: 10 MINUTES
COOK TIME: 45 MINUTES
TOTAL TIME: 55 MINUTES

METHOD

1. If using a tough meat like goat meat, place in the pot with water the same level as the meat and bring to a boil. When the meat boils for 5 minutes, add in the Plantains. If using softer meat, perhaps a soft cut of beef, put it in the pot with Plantains at the same time.
2. Once the Plantain is in the pot, add in all other ingredients except the vegetables. Let it cook for about 30 minutes on medium heat until the Plantain is thoroughly cooked. Check constantly to see if there's a need to add more water.
3. Now, add in the vegetables and let it simmer with the Plantains for 2 minutes. Turn off the heat and serve warm.

Credit: Precious Core

Oh, but just when you thought we were done with the Plantain and Porridge motif, we head to the home of one of earth's most resilient people, one of the oldest nations in the Western Hemisphere due to such resilience and eclectic Creole. None other than Papa Legba's Republic of Haiti. And no, Haiti is not an African country, but their dish, called Labouyi Bannann, is yet another Plantain porridge that fits into our Plantain Porridge theme. So here we are.

LABOUYI BANNANN

SERVINGS: 2-4

INGREDIENTS	AUTHOR'S COMMENTS
1 Green Plantain (washed)	Labouyi uses Plantains. The porridge is sweet and creamy with the consistency of light grits. Labouyi can also be made with flour and cornmeal. Try starting the day off with it.
3 Cups of Water	
1 Star Anise	
½ Cup of Evaporated Milk	
½ Cup of Coconut Milk	
½ Tsp Cinnamon Powder or 1 Stick	
¼ Cup of Sugar	
1 Tbsp of Butter	
1 Tsp Vanilla Extract	
1 Tsp Salt (Or to Taste)	

PREP TIME: 4 MINUTES
COOK TIME: 30 MINUTES
TOTAL TIME: 34 MINUTES

METHOD

1. Peel the skin of the Plantain and cut into small 4-8 pieces. It is ok to leave some of the skin for extra nutrients.
2. In a blender, puree the Plantain and 2 cups of water.
3. In a 1 quart saucepan, add 1 cup of water, evaporated milk, coconut milk, cinnamon, star anise and bring to a boil.
4. Once the pot is boiling, add the Plantain puree to the pot and bring to a boil while stirring continuously for 5 min. The porridge will thicken slightly.
5. Add the salt, sugar, vanilla and keep stirring for 10 min.
6. Reduce the heat to medium and keep stirring for another 10 min while tasting porridge to ensure the Plantain is thoroughly cooked. The porridge is ready when the texture is creamy.
7. Serve warm with some Haitian bread.

Heading closer to home to the Afro-Lusophone nations of the continent, we are starting off with the nation I have to represent, the small but mighty, São Tomé E Príncipe. Once dubbed the 'Dubai of Africa' by its former Prime Minister Patrice Trovoada, São Tomé E Príncipe is an island country formed from two archipelagos situated in the Gulf of Guinea, just off the northwestern coast of Gabon.

The Sao Tomean dish I have chosen to share with you is called Calulu de Peixe com Angu de Banana Madura. Translated to 'Fish Callaloo with Balls of Ripe Plantain.' This dish is a mixture of fish, usually garapua or cod, palm oil, tomatoes, eggplants, bay leaves, onions and more. As a dish of love and labour, we know my mum's in a good mood whenever she makes this.

CALULU DE PEIXE COM ANGU DE BANANA MADURA (FROM MY MUM)

INGREDIENTS

ANGU DE BANANA

10 Ripe Plantains (Can also be made with Unripe Green Plantains for more of a savoury taste)

3 Tbsp of Oil (Preferably a light oil)

Salt to Taste

AUTHOR'S COMMENTS

This dish can also be cooked with meat, replacing the fish. An authentic Sao Tomean Calulu will include leaves and vegetables that are grown natively on the island and difficult to access in other parts of the world. Like Ossame or Mussua leaves. For this reason, there are omissions in this recipe from the original but enough to make it taste wonderful.

The dish is cooked in two parts. The Angu de Banana (The Plantains) and the Calulu

METHOD

1. Cut and peel your Plantains, chop them into chunks and place them into a blender with a small amount of water. Add more water if necessary to help blend the mixture. Alternatively you can mash them with an appropriate utensil.
2. Once you've blended or mashed them, place the mixture into a pan on medium heat with the oil and added salt. Keep stirring the mixture until it thickens up.
3. Once it has reached a thickened consistency that has a bit of a bounce to it, take it out of the pan and if you'd like shape them into balls.
4. Serve with the chosen stew.

INGREDIENTS

CALULU DE PEIXE

1-2 portions of Smoked Fish (Cod), Pulled

1 Chopped Onion

6 Medium Sized Tomatoes, Crushed without Skins or Seeds

1 Ossame, Seeded

1 Small Chilli Pepper

1 Sprig Basil, Stems Removed and Chopped

1 Bay Leaf

1 Cup of Water

1 Cup of Wheat Flour

3-4 Garlic Cloves, Minced

3 Eggplants, Diced or Chopped

6 Okras, Stems Removed

⅓ Cup of Palm Oil

1 Tsp of Black Pepper

1 Tsp Cumin

1 Bell Pepper, Diced

250g of Fresh Spinach, Chopped

250g of Fresh Kale, Chopped

Salt to Taste

CALULU DE PEIXE (CONT.)

METHOD

1. Season your fish with salt and squeeze lemon juice over each piece and break apart the flesh. Set aside.
2. In a large pot, add the palm oil on medium-high heat. Saute the garlic and onions for a few minutes until softened.
3. Add the eggplant, tomatoes, bell peppers, okra, bay leaf and basil. Saute for about 3-5 minutes. Then add the spinach, kale and mix everything together for 2-3 minutes.
4. Add fish with the water and mix it well into the pot.
5. Lower the heat and cover the pot. Let them steam for about 20 minutes.
6. Add the flour to the mixture to thicken up the stew. Balance with water to make sure the broth is still fluid and has a stew consistency. Cook for about 5 minutes.
7. Plate the Calulu in a plate or bowl and place the Angu de Banana in the stew.

Next we go to what I would say is São Tomé's sister nation. A country and culture that we share so much in common with, where many of my uncles and aunties come from. One of the only places where Afrobeat, KFC and beer have a harmonious relationship. The country that gave American 'Gumbo' its name, deriving from the Mbundu word 'Ngombo' and where J Hus got the word 'bunda'. It is none other than Angola. In Angola there is a known dish called Mufete. The dish is a mixture of grilled fish, beans with palm oil, boiled sweet potato, cassava flour and yes, Plantain.

MUFETE

SERVINGS: 6

INGREDIENTS	AUTHOR'S COMMENTS
½ Kilo Uncooked Beans (Butter Beans or Pinto Beans)	This dish is typically Angolan. It is served on a very large plate if you add the whole fish, and put the sauce on top of the fish. On the side, place the sweet potatoes, cassava and Plantains. In a small plate, put the palm oil beans and a cup of cassava flour.
6 Whole Fishes (Traditionally Mackerels)	
1 Large Cassava	
3-4 Ripe or Unripe Plantains	
6-7 Sweet Potatoes	
2 Large Onions	
4 Garlic Cloves	
500ml Palm Oil	
1 Cup of Cassava Flour (Coarse)	
1 Tbsp Vinegar	
1 Tbsp Olive Oil	
½ Lemon (to squeeze)	
Salt to Taste	

MUFETE (CONT.)

PREP TIME: 10 MINUTES
COOK TIME: 2 HOURS 20 MINUTES
TOTAL TIME: 2 HOURS 30 MINUTES

METHOD

1. Boil the beans in a pressure pot for roughly 1 ½ hours. Then drain.
2. In the same pot, add half the palm oil with salt and let it simmer on low heat.
3. Wash and descale your fish. Then season with salt, garlic (crushed), lemon, vinegar and let it marinate for 30 minutes.
4. Grill the fish.
5. Peel the Cassava, wash it under water and boil.
6. Peel and chop the Plantains and sweet potatoes. Boil in a separate pot.
7. When all the ingredients are done cooking, combine them all on a plate/dish and serve.

Credit: Angola24horas

LATIN AMERICA

Both North and South America are home to some of the most innovative Plantain recipes my stomach aches to harbour. Named 'Plátano' across most of the region, bar Brazil, who, as part of the PALOP community, calls it 'Banana Da Terra'. The more we delve into the relationship between Plantain and Latin America the more we see just how historically ingrained the Plátano is within its wider society.

So, we start with a well known Latin American dish called Tostones, also known as 'Maduritos' in the Dominican Republic, 'Patacones' in Columbia, 'Tachinos' in Cuba and 'Bannann Peze' in Haiti. Like many other Plantain dishes, Tostones are Plantains fried in oil. They are cooked and claimed by so many nations, it's hard to authentically attribute it to one country. Supposedly originating in either the Dominican Republic or Puerto Rico (but this is regularly disputed and debated), the origin of the name is believed to lie between the word 'toston' referring to an antiquated coin used in Latin America, which tostones sort of look like, and the term 'toston' relating to the Portuguese word for 'toasted'.

So what's so different between Tostones and other fried Plantain? It's quite simple. Tostones are fried twice. Fried once, then smashed with swift precision and fried again. This double frying method is sometimes used by chefs making french fries. While the act of double frying may threaten the acquisition of any nutritional value that Plantains have to offer, it does taste bloody brilliant!

Like I mentioned before, in some parts of the continent, like Venezuela and Columbia, Tostones may be called something else. In the case of both countries, the alternative name is 'Patacones'. Johnny Ventura, an Afro-Dominican singer, former mayor and vice mayor of Santa Domingo, with one

TOSTONES

SERVINGS: 4

INGREDIENTS	AUTHOR'S COMMENTS
2 Unripe Plantains (Green)	Tostones (Dominican Twice-Fried Plantains): without a doubt, one of our favorite side dishes. With a very crispy texture, it is vastly preferred to French fries.
½ Cup Oil	
Salt to Taste	

OPTIONAL DIP

1 Ripe Tomato, Chopped	
4 Sprigs of Parsley	
1 Tsp Pepper	
1 Tbsp Olive Oil	

PREP TIME: 5 MINUTES
COOK TIME: 10 MINUTES
TOTAL TIME: 15 MINUTES

METHOD

1. Peel the Plantains and cut into 1 inch (2.5cm) thick slices.
2. In a deep frying pan, heat the oil over medium heat and fry the Plantains till they're a light golden colour. (Roughly 5 mins)
3. Flatten the Plantains using a 'tostonera' (can buy on Amazon) or a cup.
4. Place the flattened Plantains back into the frying pan and fry again until they're a golden yellow again. (Roughly 5 minutes)
5. Drain the tostones on paper towels if necessary and serve with sprinkles of salt while hot.

Credit: Dominican Cooking

of the coolest names ever once made a very passionate song about how he wants nothing more than for his wife to make him Patacon Pisao.

The only difference between 'Tostones' and 'Patacones' is that 'Patacones' usually come jumbo-sized.

Next on the Plantain dish list, we have a dish that can only be described as a Plantain sandwich. A sandwich known as the Jibarito. Pronounced differently to how you probably first said it, the Jibarito is pronounced 'Hee-ba-rito'. It's likely the Jibarito derives its name from the term 'Jibaro', which I've mentioned before in this book, and describes the figurative agricultural workers of Puerto Rico, who, through the imagery of the Jibaro, represents the rich heritage and positive culture of Puerto Rico.

The Jibarito, according to legend (somewhere on the internet), is the original Plátano sandwich.

It was born in Chicago in 1996 where the imprint of the Hispanic diaspora on America's social strata and makeup was, and remains, huge. The creation of the Jibarito is credited to a man named Juan Peter Figueroa, who, after multiple Google searches, seems to be a bit of a Batman figure. Looming in online anonymity, he isn't as visible as his apparent inventions are. The legend goes: Juan, a Puerto Rican, was inspired after reading about a Puerto Rican sandwich in the *El Vocero* newspaper and thought he'd try his hand at it and struck Plantain gold.

Till this day, the jibarito is celebrated as one of 'Chicago's Greatest Food[6] inventions'.

JIBARITO OR JIBARITA

SERVINGS: 4

INGREDIENTS	AUTHOR'S COMMENTS
2 Tbsp of Oil	The distinguishing feature of this sandwich is the replacement of bread with smashed, fried plantains. It's brilliantly delicious and you can add any of your favorite sandwich fixings.
2 Large Green Plantains	
¼ Cup of Mayonnaise	
¼ Tsp of Chilli Powder	
¼ Tsp of Cumin Powder	This particular jibarito recipe features roast beef topped with Swiss cheese, lettuce, tomato, and a spiced mayonnaise. You can make these full-sized and enjoy them as a meal or cut the plantains down and build them into small party sandwiches.
¼ Tsp of Garlic Powder	
4 Handfuls of Lettuce	
1 Tomato, Thinly Sliced	
1 Onion, Peeled and Cut into Slivers	It is important to use green plantains, as they are firm enough to resemble bread, whereas yellow (and definitely black) would be too soft.
4 Slices of Swiss Cheese	
¼ Pound of Roast Beef, Thinly Sliced	Ensure the plantain slices are fried until they're nice and crispy and are drained very well, otherwise, you will end up with a greasy mess.
Olives for Garnish	If you scour Chicago's restaurant menus, you will find jibaritos with everything from chicken to shrimp and even vegetarian versions with tofu. Whatever you choose, be sure to top it with a great cheese and the freshest, crispest vegetables you can find.
	You can increase or decrease the size of this recipe to fit your needs. Simply keep in mind that one plantain will make two full sandwiches.

JIBARITO OR JIBARITA (CONT.)

PREP TIME: 19 MINUTES
COOK TIME: 12 MINUTES
TOTAL TIME: 31 MINUTES

METHOD

1. Gather all of your ingredients first before cooking.
2. Heat the oil to 375 F°.
3. Peel the Plantains, cut them in half and then cut each half lengthwise.
4. Fry the Plantains in oil for 4 minutes. Remove from hot oil and drain on paper towels.
5. Flatten the Plantains. Re-fry in the hot oil for another 4 minutes until the Plantains are crispy. Remove from the oil and drain on paper towels. Then set aside.
6. In a small bowl, mix together the mayonnaise, chilli powder, cumin powder, and garlic powder.
7. Spread the mayonnaise mix on one side of the flat Plantains.
8. Build your sandwich by layering the tomatoes, onions, cheese and roast beef, using the flat Plantains as if it were bread.
9. Stick a toothpick with olives in the middle of the sandwich and serve immediately.

Credit: The Spruce Eats

Before leaving Puerto Rico, we sample another dish from their cuisine, which, in translation, might raise a few eyebrows, but it is nothing to worry about. Named Arañitas de Plátano, this next dish gets its name from the Spanish word for spiders, 'arañas', in reference to the dish's appearance of loads of little spider legs stuck together. Enjoyed as a Puerto Rican snack or as ~~a side dish~~ an appetizer because Plantain can never be a side ting.

ARAÑITAS

INGREDIENTS	AUTHOR'S COMMENTS
3-4 Green Plantains Garlic Salt to Taste	These arañitas or spiders are a Puerto Rican invention and act as a substitute for the traditional tostones; If you would like to avoid frying, you can bake the arañitas in the oven at 350°F for 20 minutes. As an alternative, you can use green bananas when preparing this recipe.

PREP TIME: 10 MINUTES
COOK TIME: 15 MINUTES
TOTAL TIME: 25 MINUTES

METHOD

1. Start by peeling the Plantains, then take the interior portions and grate like a piece of cheese (into strips). Season with garlic salt as desired.
2. Heat a sufficient amount of oil for frying in a skillet over medium-high heat. To prepare the aranitas, take approximately one or two tablespoons of the grated Plantains and smash the 'strips' together between your hands.
3. Fry the aranitas on each side until golden brown. When ready, remove from the oil and let sit over a paper towel to remove any excess oil.

Credit: Que Rica Vida

Then there is the Mofongo, which, like a lot of cuisine across Latin America, can be traced back to West Africa. The Mofongo is a staple food in many Puerto Rican and Dominican households. The style in which Mofongo is made takes its influence from a style of cooking heavily affiliated with African cuisine. The style of boiling, pounding, mashing and expanding starchy foods is used to make dishes like Fufu or the aforementioned Foutou Banane. Through the arrival of African slaves on the continent, this typically West African style of cooking was introduced but instead of yam, it was used on the most accessible starch of the land. Plantain. So Puerto Rican Mofongo and other styles of dishes like it including the Dominican Mangu, Colombian Cayeye or Peruvian Tacacho, are essentially Hispanic fufu with insular evolutions.

So here's to Mofongo, Mangu, Cayeye, Tacacho and the other variations.

TRADITIONAL PLANTAIN MOFONGO	
SERVINGS: 4	
INGREDIENTS	**AUTHOR'S COMMENTS**
2 Cups of Vegetable Oil, for Frying	To make mofongo, the Plantains are sliced and fried until tender, and then mashed with garlic paste and pork cracklings. The mixture can either be formed into balls or a half-dome shape. Mofongo is traditionally mashed in a mortar and pestle, but you can use a potato masher if you don't have one.
3 Medium Green, Unripe Plantains	
1 Tbsp Garlic Paste	
6 Ounces of Pork Rings or Cracklings, Crushed	Mofongo is a side dish as well as the main course, especially when it is stuffed with meat or seafood. It can be accompanied by a protein, such as chicken or shrimp, and by beans and rice, but is also often presented in a bowl with a broth poured over the top. The Puerto Rican dish is also served directly out of the mortar.

Credit: The Spruce Eats: Hector Rodriguez

TRADITIONAL PLANTAIN MOFONGO (CONT.)

PREP TIME: 10 MINUTES
COOK TIME: 5 MINUTES
TOTAL: 15 MINUTES

METHOD

1. Gather all of your ingredients first before cooking.
2. Heat about 2 inches of oil in a frying pan or deep fryer to 350 F°.
3. While the oil is heating up, peel the Plantains and cut into 1-inch rounds.
4. Fry the Plantains until golden and tender. This will take approximately 4 to 6 minutes.
5. Remove cooked Plantains from the pan or fryer and allow to drain on paper towels.
6. Put the garlic paste in a mixing or mortar and add the fried Plantains. Mash until thoroughly blended.
7. Add the pork rinds. Continue to mash and mix until all of the ingredients are well incorporated.
8. Shape the mofongo into 4 balls.
9. Alternatively, you can make the mofongo into a half-dome shape using a small condiment bowl as a mold; push a portion of mofongo down to the bottom of the bowl.
10. With the back of a spoon smooth over and level off the mix.
11. Then use the spoon to scrape around the bowl and remove the mash in a half-dome shape.
12. Serve the mofongo hot and enjoy.

MANGU

SERVINGS: 4

INGREDIENTS	AUTHOR'S COMMENTS
4 Unripe Plantains	Mangú (Mashed Plantains) is one of the best known and most representative dishes of Dominican cuisine. It could probably be called The Dominican Republic's Official Breakfast Dish.
1 ½ Tsp of Salt	
4 Tbsp Olive Oil, or Butter	
1 Cup of Water	

ONION GARNISH

2 Tbsp of Olive Oil	
2 Red Onions, Large	
1 Tbsp Fruit Vinegar	
Salt to Taste	

MANGU (CONT.)

PREP TIME: 15 MINUTES
COOK TIME: 20 MINUTES
TOTAL TIME: 35 MINUTES

METHOD

1. Peel the Plantains and cut lengthwise, then divide each half into two. Remove the center where the seeds are located (optional for a smoother mangu).
2. Boil the Plantains in enough water to cover them plus an inch until they are very tender, having added the salt to the water before the water breaks the boil.
3. Remove the Plantains from the water and mash them right away with a fork until they are very smooth and there are few to no lumps. Mix in the olive oil and water at room temperature and keep mashing, mixing until it turns into a smooth puree.

ONIONS

1. Heat a tablespoon of oil in a skillet over low heat. Add onions and cook, stir until they become translucent. Pour in vinegar and season with salt to taste.
2. Garnish the Mangu with the onions and serve with sunny-side up eggs or Dominican scrambled eggs, Dominican fried cheese or fried slices of Dominican salami.

Credit: Dominican Cooking

COLOMBIAN CAYEYE AND HOGAO

SERVINGS: 3-4

INGREDIENTS	AUTHOR'S COMMENTS
2 Green Plantains, Peeled	Pronounced 'kay-yah-yah' and 'oh-gou' this simple yet very nutritious breakfast is fresh and fragrant. It starts with a bed of boiled and mashed Plantains, cayeye, which is then topped with hogao, a popular Colombian relish made from tomatoes, green onions, garlic, and cumin. To finish it off, an egg is most often served on top. Although often eaten at breakfast, it is also very acceptable for dinner.
Water for Boiling	
2 Tsp Olive Oil	
2 Roma Tomatoes, Diced	
2 Bunches of Green Onion, Chopped	
2 Garlic Cloves, Minced	
½ Tsp Cumin	
½ Tsp Sea Salt	
½ Tsp Ground Pepper	
3-4 Eggs	

METHOD

1. Boil the green Plantain for 20 minutes, then mash with ¼ cup of the boiling water until smooth.
2. For the *Hogao:* In a skillet, add a few tablespoons of olive oil and saute the onions, garlic, salt, pepper and cumin for a few minutes just until fragrant, over medium-low heat.
3. Next, add the tomatoes and saute for a couple more minutes until everything is warm and slightly soft, but not mushy.
4. Plate the mashed Plantains, with salt and pepper as desired, topped with the hogao.
5. Fry on the egg for each dish, to the desire of the consumer. Sunny-side up or over-easy are two popular options.
6. Place the egg on top of the hogao for each dish and enjoy.

Credit: SemiSeriousChefs

TACACHO

INGREDIENTS	AUTHOR'S COMMENTS
4 Green Plantains	One of the most popular dishes of the gastronomy of the Peruvian jungle is the tacacho with cecina. This delicacy is usually enjoyed during the Fiesta de San Juan, a typical jungle festival. This dessert is prepared with bellaco Verde Plantain; this can be cooked fried, roasted, or parboiled; in the traditional preparation, sajino chicharrón is used instead of jerky. This dish consists of two balls of tacacho, the jerky, and chorizo; however, the dish's proportion may vary depending on each one.
400 Gr of Bacon or Pork Rinds	
½ Cup Oil	
Salt to Taste	
	It is a dish that originated in the Peruvian jungle. Its name probably comes from the Quechua 'taka chu,' which means 'the beaten', which refers to the banana, which is a characteristic ingredient of tacacho with jerky, is crushed.

METHOD

1. Peel the Plantains and cut them in half lengthwise. Boil them in a pot for about 20 minutes.
2. Once cooked, remove them from the pot and crush them in a bowl with the help of a utensil (preferably made of wood so the mixture doesn't stick). Once done, add salt to taste and continue to mix.
3. Heat a frying pan and add the oil. Fry or poach the bacon or pork rinds (cut into cubes).
4. Mix into the Plantain mixture with the remaining oil and set aside.
5. Let the mixture cool enough to separate and mold into 4 balls with your hands.
6. Serve chosen sides.

The Pastelón is the Hispanic Plantain's take on the lasagne. When you search 'Pastelón' by itself you'll see the dish credited to Puerto Rican cuisine. However, when you search 'Pastelón de Plátano Maduro' more results will show you its origin in Dominican cuisine. I've even seen recipes dedicating the dish to Venezuela. Each as alluring and dazzling as each other.

I will be going for the Dominican variety here.

PASTELÓN DE PLÁTANO MADURO

SERVINGS: 6

INGREDIENTS	AUTHOR'S COMMENTS
FOR THE FILLING	Plantains are accused, no less, of being partly responsible for our island's rampant underdevelopment. It is said to block the brain and stop intelligence from flowing, according to some; while others say overindulgence leads to a dazed stupor. (Won't stop you from eating them anyway).
2 Tbsp Olive Oil	
1 Red Onion, Minced	
3 Cloves of Garlic, Crushed or Minced	
1 lb Minced Beef	Aside from Mangú, Pastelón de Plátano Maduro (Ripe Plantain Casserole) is possibly the second most popular Plantain recipe in the DR. A dish that nearly no Dominican will turn down.
1 Cup Tomato Sauce	
1 Seeded and Minced Bell Pepper	
Salt to Taste	
Black Pepper to Taste	
1 Tsp Chopped Cilantro or Parsley	
TO ASSEMBLE	
6 Very Ripe Plantains, (Black or Yellow going Black)	
1 Tsp Salt	
¼ Cup Butter	
1 Cup Grated Cheddar Cheese (Your Cheese of Choice)	

PASTELÓN DE PLÁTANO MADURO (CONT.)

PREP TIME: 15 MINUTES
COOK TIME: 45 MINUTES
TOTAL TIME: 60 MINUTES

METHOD

FOR THE FILLING

1. Heat oil over medium-low heat. Stir in onion and cook and stir until it turns translucent. Add garlic and cook, stirring for a minute.
2. Add minced meat and cook and stir, breaking into small clumps until it browns.
3. Pour in tomato sauce, add bell pepper, salt and pepper. Stir and cover. Simmer for 3 minutes.
4. Uncover and mix in the optional ingredient of your choice or none at all if you so prefer.
5. Taste and season with salt and pepper to taste if needed. Remove from the heat.

TO ASSEMBLE

1. Peel and boil the Plantains, adding a 1 tsp of salt to the water and let them boil for 15-29 minutes until they are tender.
2. Take the Plantains out of the water right away and mash them with a fork. Add the butter and keep mashing until they are smooth with no lumps.
3. Grease a 1 inch tall baking pan. Put half of the Plantain mixture in the baking pan. Cover with half of the cheese.
4. Bake in a preheated oven to 175 C° until the top is golden brown.
5. Let it cool and serve.

Credit: Dominican Cooking

Next up, we have Pasteles (Puerto Rican) and Pasteles de Maduro (Dominican). These recipes take from a Mesoamerican dish called Tamale. However, they also strike a resemblance with another recipe in our trove of Plantain dishes, Empanadas. Found all over the region, Empanadas are like baked pockets of goodness with heart-fulfilling fillings, traditionally wrapped around with gorgeous bread. The Spanish word 'empanar' translates to 'enbreaded', however, instead of bread Empanadas de Plátano are wrapped in Plantain, in a similar way to the Pasteles.

I've chosen to go with the Colombian variety here:

EMPANADAS DE PLÁTANO MADURO Y QUESOS
SERVINGS: 6
INGREDIENTS
4 Very Ripe Plantains
1 Egg
2 Tbsp Butter
3 Tbsp All-Purpose Flour
½ Tsp Vanilla Extract
1 Tbsp sugar
1 Cup Mozzarella Cheese (or cheese of choice), Grated
Oil spray for cooking

EMPANADAS DE PLÁTANO MADURO Y QUESO (CONT.)

METHOD

1. Wash and cut the Plantains in half. Cook them with the skin on over medium-high heat in a large pot with water, until Plantains are cooked and soft. About 10 minutes.
2. Peel and mash the cooked Plantains with a fork or a potato masher until you get a soft mixture. Let it rest for 5 minutes.
3. Add the egg, butter, flour, vanilla extract and sugar. Mix well into each other.
4. Form the dough into a ball and let it rest in a bowl at room temperature for about 20 minutes. Form 12 balls with the Plantain dough and press down each ball to make a disc with the palm of your hand.
5. Add the cheese in the middle, fold the dough in half and press to seal with your fingers, or use a fork to help seal the edges so the cheese is sealed and does not melt out.
6. Spray oil on a baking sheet or cover with wax paper. Preheat the oven to 400 F° or 204 C°.
7. Place the empanadas on the baking sheet in the oven for about 15 minutes, then turn the empanadas and cook for about 15 minutes more until golden.
8. Serve warm.

Credit: My Colombian Recipes

THE CARIBBEAN

Okay so now we head over to the West Indies. The islands that gave us the fastest man on earth, the sounds of calypso, reggae, soca, dancehall, half of the Black culture across the globe and for what it's worth, the only pirate in history to be surnamed 'Plantain'. Where you don't 'over do it'. You ova dweet.

And as much as it galls the West African jingoist in me to consider saying 'Plantin' over Plantain. I want everyone reading these next few paragraphs, even you, my West African broda, to practice the 'Plantin' pronunciation in respect to the islands.

In Trinidad and Tobago, there is a much loved Plantain-looking delicacy called Moko, not to be confused with the bacterial disease that kills off a number of banana and Plantain plantations. It cooks like Plantains and looks like Plantains, only small and usually fatter. Botanically speaking, they aren't Plantains but can be considered in our 'faux-Plantain' category. You can fry Moko like you would Plantain for an enjoyable faux-Plantain experience.

For the next two recipes we're going over to a Caribbean nation that needs no introduction: Jamaica. The influence the Jamaican diaspora have had all over the world from pop-culture, sports and music to arts and politics is huge.

When it comes to Plantain, much about its place in Jamaican cuisine is presumed to be simple. Bit of oil, bit of heat, slice, dice, slap it in the oil and dazzit. I am here to tell you there is more to Plantain in Jamaican cuisine than meets the eye. So, here's two takes on Plantain that you may not have been blessed with yet, first on the list is actual Plantain Porridge.

PLANTAIN PORRIDGE

SERVINGS: 4

INGREDIENTS	AUTHOR'S COMMENTS
1 Large Green Plantain (Washed, peeled and chopped in quarters)	Plantain porridge is one of Jamaica's favourites, made with Green Plantain, milk and spices. For this recipe I'm using fresh coconut milk, but you can use whatever milk that suits you.
2 Cups of Fresh Coconut Milk	
1 Cinnamon Stick (Or 2 cinnamon leaves)	Plantain porridge is high fibre and a great source of carbohydrates, keeping you full all morning.
¼ Tsp Freshly grated nutmeg	
1 Tsp Vanilla extract	Use one cup of water if you like your porridge to be thick. I like mine a little runny.
¼ Tsp Salt	
1 ½ Cup Water	Instead of a cinnamon stick or leaf, you can also use ground cinnamon.
Condensed Milk	

PREP TIME: 5 MINUTES
COOK TIME: 10 MINUTES
TOTAL TIME: 15 MINUTES

METHOD

1. In a blender, add the Plantain, grated nutmeg, along with one cup and a half of coconut milk. Blend until smooth.
2. Add the water to a pot with the cinnamon stick (or leaves) and salt. Leave to boil on medium heat.
3. Once the water is boiled, pour the blended mixture into the boiling water. Stir continuously.
4. Add the rest of the coconut milk.
5. As the porridge starts thickening, turn the heat down.
6. Let the porridge cook for 5 to 10 minutes.
7. Add the vanilla and sweeten to taste with condensed milk.

Credit: Jamaican Food Recipes: Lesa

The second offering from Jamaica is the Plantain Tart, which looks like a dessert take on the patty, offering serious sweetness.

JAMAICAN PLANTAIN TART	
SERVINGS: 4	
INGREDIENTS	**AUTHOR'S COMMENTS**
White Sugar for Decoration	A delicious dessert filled with a sweet flavour ready to tantalize your taste buds. A union between dough and ripe Plantain like you've never encountered.
1 Egg White, Beaten	
2 Drops of Red Food Colouring (Optional)	
1 Tsp Grated Nutmeg	
1 Tsp Vanilla Extract	
¼ Cup White Sugar	
3 Very Ripe Plantains (Black)	
FOR FILLING	
1 Tbsp Ice Cold Water	
1 Egg, Beaten	
3 Tbsp Shortening, Chilled and Diced	
¼ Cup Cold Butter, Cut Into ½ Inch Pieces	
1 Tsp Salt	
2 Cups All Purpose Flour	
Ingredients Pastry	

JAMAICAN PLANTAIN TART (CONT.)

PREP TIME: 20 MINUTES
COOK TIME: 25 MINUTES
TOTAL: 45 MINUTES

METHOD

1. Prepare the pastry by combining the flour and salt in a bowl.
2. Rub in the butter and shortening until incorporated, and the mixture takes on a sandy appearance.
3. Combine the egg and water, and stir into the flour mixture until a dough forms, then knead for a few turns to bring the dough together.
4. Wrap well and chill for 3 hours in the refrigerator.
5. While the dough is chilling, peel Plantains and cut into thirds. Place into a small saucepan with a little water.
6. Bring to a simmer and steam until tender, 5 to 10 minutes depending on how ripe your Plantains are.
7. Once soft, pour out the water and mash Plantains with sugar, vanilla, nutmeg and red food colouring. Set aside to cool.
8. Preheat the oven to 350 F (175 C).
9. Roll dough out on a lightly floured surface to 1/4 inch thick.
10. Cut into circles using a 4 or 5 inch round cookie cutter or similar utensil.
11. Spoon a little of the Plantain filling into the center of each circle, then fold in half, to form a half-moon shape.
12. Place the tarts on a baking sheet, brush with beaten egg white, and sprinkle with sugar.
13. Bake in a preheated oven for 20 to 25 minutes until golden brown. Allow tarts to cool to room temperature before serving.

Credit: Jamaican Bikkle

ASIA

Now we will be looking at a region that is less associated with Plantain. South Asia. Despite the fact that the musaceae diversification in South Asia is plentiful, Plantain popularity is not.

For starters, we will explore what is called the Saba banana, sometimes called the Saging Saba. From the Philippines, the Saba is a banana cultivar that comes in at an average size of 7–13 centimeters and whilst biologically the Saba isn't a Plantain, it acts and looks exactly like a Plantain. Just a lot smaller with slightly less starch.

What's most interesting about Saba is the ways in which it is used. Unlike the Caribbean or the African Plantain, which are used more often for savoury recipes, in the Philippines the Saba is used as a main ingredient for wonderfully sweet and sugary desserts.

Starting with a simple and classic Saba dish, Minatamis Na Saging, which roughly translates to 'Sweet Banana'. Minatamis Saba is a dish that tries not to do too much. Instead, it works to amplify the sweetness of Saba through the process of caramelization. For those of us without access to Saba, a ripe Plantain can be used.

MINATAMIS NA SAGING	
SERVINGS: 4	
INGREDIENTS	**AUTHOR'S COMMENTS**
4 Pieces of Saba Banana (Plantain)	Minatamis Na Saging is a dessert dish wherein Plantains (locally known as 'saging na saba') are sweetened by cooking in a sweet mixture composed of water, brown sugar, salt, and vanilla extract.
¾ Cup Brown Sugar	
1 ½ Cups Water	
1 Tsp Vanilla Extract	This is one of the quick and easy Filipino dessert recipes that we have. Imagine making your own dessert in less than 15 minutes; you can use your extra time in trying our other dessert recipes.
¼ Tsp Salt	

PREP TIME: 10 MINUTES
COOK TIME: 30 MINUTES
TOTAL TIME: 40 MINUTES

METHOD

1. Heat a cooking pot and pour in water, then let boil.
2. Add brown sugar and stir until diluted.
3. Add salt and vanilla extract and mix well.
4. Put in the Plantains, peeled and cut in half if necessary. Adjust the heat to medium and cover the cooking pot and simmer for 8 to 12 minutes or until the liquid thickens.
5. Turn off heat and allow the Plantains to cool.

Credit: Panlasangpinoy

Carrying on with this theme of slight yet culturally critical variation, the Ginanggang, or Guinangang, is a dish that is best described as Saba or Mini Plantain Skewers. Ginanggang's origin lies in the island of Mindanao in the Philippines, which has a long Spanish colonial history.

Here's the dish.

GINANGGANG

INGREDIENTS	AUTHOR'S COMMENTS
Saba Banana (or Plantain), peeled and skewered.	This is Ginanggang. Ginanggang is a snack food of grilled skewered bananas brushed with margarine and sprinkled with sugar. This particular snack is very popular in Mindanao where it originated. Enjoy this recipe from all of us at Filipino Chow.
Margarine	
Sugar	

METHOD

1. Fire up the grill.
2. When the grill is nice and hot, place the skewered Sabas or Plantains, cut in half on the grill.
3. Brush each Saba/Plantain with margarine and sprinkle with sugar or roll each Saba/Plantain on a plate full of sugar.
4. Serve while hot.

Credit: Filipino Chow

Moving on to another sweet and delectable dish, loved in Tagalog-speaking Filipino culture is the Turon. Etymologically, it's easy to connect Turon with Spanish origin because the word 'Turron' also refers to a spanish candy-like food. The snack can be best described as a spring roll because of its style, but there's nothing remotely savoury about it.

TURON

SERVINGS: 10 TURONS

INGREDIENTS	AUTHOR'S COMMENTS
3-4 Medium Sized Ripe Plantains (Cut in half), or 5 Saba Bananas	Turon is a classic Filipino snack made with a slice of banana that is then rolled in brown sugar, wrapped and fried. The typical type of banana used in this snack is Saba (burro banana). Sometimes other fruits are used along with the banana, such as jackfruit or mango. Furthermore, turon is considered a street food in the Philippines and you can see this delicious snack sold on the streets along with other favorites like banana cue.
4 Tbsp Dark Brown Sugar	
1 Cup Vegetable Oil	
10 8-inch Frozen Spring Roll Wrapper, Thawed and Separated	
Vanilla Ice Cream (For serving)	It's best to use very ripe Plantains in replacement for Saba bananas.

PREP TIME: 10 MINUTES
COOK TIME: 10 MINUTES
TOTAL: 20 MINUTES

METHOD

1. Prepare the bananas. Whether using Plantains or Saba, peel and slice in half lengthwise. Set aside.
2. Spread the brown sugar on a shallow dish.
3. Lay a wrapper on a plate with 1 corner facing you. Thoroughly cover 1 slice of Plantains/Saba in sugar and then place it along the corner of the wrapper closest to you. Roll the wrapper over the Plantains/Saba, tuck in both sides and roll it up tight. Moisten the end with water and press to seal. Repeat the process with the rest of the Saba/Plantain.
4. Heat the oil in a frying pan over medium high heat. Fry the turon, in batches until golden brown, about 3 minutes per batch. Drain on paper towels.
5. Serve as is or with vanilla ice cream.

Credit: (Salu Salo: Liza Agbanlog)

To finish up, we are going to look at the Maruya. The Maruya is just a banana fritter. In fact I'd go as far as saying they are two peas in a pod, two fritters in a pan. The Maruya is another merienda snack and it also finds itself on street markets sold by street vendors all over the Philippines.

MARUYA

INGREDIENTS	AUTHOR'S COMMENTS
1 Cup Flour	To prepare 'pinaypay-style', cut each saba (or Plantain) vertically into three to five slices without going all the way through on one end.
½ Cup Sugar	
1 Tsp Baking Powder	
¼ Tsp Salt	Carefully spread the slices to make a 'fan' and dip in the batter to coat.
1 Egg	
1 Cup Cold Milk	The fritters take about 1 to 2 minutes to cook per each side.
2 Tbsp Butter, Melted	
Canola Oil	Once bubbles appear on the top of the fritter and the bottom is golden brown, carefully flip to the other side, and continue to cook until browned.
6 Ripe but Firm Saba Bananas (Or Plantains), peeled and sliced lengthwise into about ¼ inch thick pieces	

PREP TIME: 15 MINUTES
COOK TIME: 10 MINUTES
TOTAL TIME: 25 MINUTES

METHOD

1. In a bowl, sift together flour, ¼ cup of the sugar, baking powder, and salt.
2. In a large bowl, beat the egg.
3. Add milk and butter and whisk together until blended.
4. Add flour mixture to milk mixture and stir until just moistened. *Do not over mix*
5. In a pan over medium heat, heat the oil.
6. Dip the Saba/Plantain slices into batter to fully coat and gently slide into hot oil. Cook for about 1 to 2 minutes on each side or until golden and crisp.
7. Remove from the pan and drain on paper towels.
8. Using a fine-mesh sieve, dust the maruya with the remaining sugar and serve while warm.

Credit: Kawaling Pinoy: Lalaine Manalo

Wait. There's yet another country that embraces the greatness of Plantain and also lays claim to the banana fritter. From India, this dish is called the Pazham Pori. The dish, sometimes called Ethakka Appam, looks like what you might expect of a Southeastern take on a banana fritter. Bathed deep in oil and served with Chaya Tea, crispy all around the outside and soft in the middle.

PAZHAM PORI (ALSO CALLED ETHAKKA APPAM)	
INGREDIENTS	**AUTHOR'S COMMENTS**
2 Ripe Plantains	Pazham Pori is an all time favourite snack of malayalees. It is also called "Ethakka Appam". It is an easy to prepare snack which does not require any great cooking experience. People usually use all purpose flour, but you can also use atta flour if you are more health conscious.
1 Cup All Purpose Flour	
1 Tbsp Rice Flour	
1 Tbsp Sugar	
1 Pinch Turmeric Powder (Optional)	
¾ Water	Instead of rice flour, you can use Semolina as an alternative. It is mainly used to make Pazham Pori more crispy.
Salt to Taste	
Oil to Deep Fry	

METHOD

1. Peel the Plantains and slit it lengthwise.
2. In a bowl, take all the purpose flour, rice flour, sugar, turmeric powder and salt. Blend it nicely by adding ¾ cup of water.
3. Dip the Plantain slices in the prepared batter and evenly coat them.
4. Heat the oil in a deep bottom pan. When it is hot, deep fry the batter coated Plantain slices by turning both sides till golden brown.
5. Serve the Pazham Pori hot with a cup of tea after draining the excess oil using a paper towel.

Credit: Tasty Circle: Shaan Geo

We could keep going. There seems to be no limit to Plantain's variety. Whether in the East or the West, from the Caribbean to Africa down to Asia, Plantain and all its children are in somebody's kitchen working hard to provide satisfaction. From desserts to dinners, breakfasts to snacks. Plantain serves as a go-to cooking essential in plenty of national cuisines far and wide. A fruit of the world.

6

THE POLITICAL CRINKUM CRANKUM OF PLANTAIN

So, remember when I mentioned the United Fruit Company? This next story starts with them.

Before bananas were brought over from the Caribbean, no one in the West had ever seen a fruit shipped over the ocean. The United Fruit Company, under the leadership of its founders, Andrew Preston and Minor Cooper Keith, used a network of ice-cooled warehouses, boxcars and ships, vertically integrating the whole operation in a way that paralleled oil and steel monopolies. Just with bananas.[1]

Preston had predicted that bananas could become more popular than apples—and he was right. Decades of aggressive advertising campaigns—including tactics such as distributing whole manuals to schoolchildren on the nutritional benefits of bananas—gradually enshrined the fruit as a wholesome, fundamental part of the American diet.[2]

The popularity of bananas rose so much that people were literally slipping on banana peels discarded through the streets. It got so bad that in 1909, the city of St. Louis, Missouri, had to outlaw 'throwing or casting' a banana peel out in public. It was in fact this banana-slipping epidemic that supposedly birthed the famous banana-slipping comedy gag that you may have seen in classic cartoons and Charlie Chaplin skits.[3]

By the early 1900s, the banana had outsold both apples and

oranges in the US.[4] When the US government tried to impose a banana tax to cream off the amount the fruit was being consumed, the United Fruit Company stepped in and fought against it, keeping the fruit cheap as the 'fruit of the people'.[5] It's an interesting parallel with the current rise of Plantain prices being a conversation that seems to only be happening within Black and Brown communities. A conversation we'll get more into later.

Things weren't too dissimilar in Britain either. Harry Roy, a dance band leader and performer from Stamford Hill, London, known for a song that predates modern rap songs— his 1931 smash hit 'My Girl's P*ssy'—also made a song detailing how much excitement there was around the banana, with his stand out song 'When Can I Have A Banana Again?'.

Even OBE comedic singer and poet Stanley Holloway felt the fever, naming his 1958 record album *Let's Have A Banana*. And so, yuppies* and working-class folk alike, all over the city, were consuming the fruit like crazy.

Granted. The banana was also later used to subject Black people to racism. Becoming a tool to relay racist themes throughout the country. In 1923, Pulitzer prize winner Wallace Stevens had used bananas in his poem 'Floral Decoration for Bananas' to epitomize white women as precious and elegant, like plums, and Black women, ogre-like and noxious, like hacked, hunched and musky bananas growing out of their purple craws.[6] Not to mention the countless times banana peels have been thrown at Black sports stars, politicians and celebrities to reduce and remind them of their supposed racial inferiority.

Arriving both in Europe and America around the early 1600s, dessert bananas had plenty of time to properly enter

---

*   A fashionable young middle-class person with a well-paid job, mostly associated with the 1980s.

and flourish British and American markets. By the late 1800s–early 1900s, the introduction of accessible refrigeration for traders working with global products[7] meant the fruit's popularity went from strength to strength as it became much easier for the supply of bananas to meet the global demand. Even William Cavendish, the Sixth Duke of Devonshire, felt the urge to attach his legacy to the fruit, cultivating his own variety of the fruit and naming it the 'Cavendish'. Which is the variety of banana we are most familiar with today.

During this period of the banana becoming the 'it' fruit, the United Fruit Company was operating in Costa Rica and parts of the Caribbean as early as 1890. They also had access to Plantain produce, creating the economy for Plantain exports that countries like Colombia and Ecuador rely on today. In comparison to the dessert banana, Plantain was probably just as, if not better, suited for being moved across borders.

And while they were marketed differently in different periods, Plantains and bananas were 'discovered' in Africa by Europeans and brought to the West around the same time. The introduction of the Musa species in America and the UK was made by botanists like Carl Linnaeus and John Gerard who saw the value in all varieties of the species. The latter of whom, some suspect, actually presented Plantains, and not bananas, in his known 1633 drawing entitled 'Herball or Generall Historie of Plantes' (general history of plants).[8] This confounding of Plantain with the banana, persists throughout popular culture and works to mute Plantain's presence in regions throughout America and the UK.

Why is all of this important anyway? Well, it is sort of my disclaimer. A long one at that. So that you know, when I start talking about the early political developments of Plantain, it's inevitable that it'll actually be enveloped within wider conversations

PLANTAIN
WORD
COUNT:
828

about early developments of the banana as well. The two are interlinked.

POLITICS OF THE BANANA: UNITED FRUIT COMPANY, BANANA REPUBLIC AND FARMING

The political story of Plantain that concerns the eaters of the fruit today, starts with the United Fruit Company. The company that inspired the term 'Banana Republic'. The 'Banana Republic' was coined in the 1904 book *Cabbages and Kings* by William Sydney Porter. Porter first used the term to refer not to luxury garments as some of you may have assumed, but to the nature of the economic exploitation in countries like Honduras by the American company, the United Fruit Company.

Wanted by the US for bank embezzlement, Porter lived in Honduras for roughly 6 months until he was caught hiding in a hotel.[9] Brought to prison in the US, he came up with the pen name O. Henry and started writing about his experiences in Honduras. His story in all is not that important but his experiences in Honduras are. As an American man in a new country, he observed the Honduran way of life. One of the things he looked on, in more of a satirical way, was the reality of a foreign fruit company, that in his eyes had more control and governance in the country than their national government had.

That company was, of course, the United Fruit Company.

From the late 1800s to the late 1900s, the United Fruit Company operated in and around the Caribbean and South America in a capacity that looked a lot like the Spanish and English colonies. Throughout South America and the

Caribbean, American and British businessmen were, to put it simply, taking the piss. Using financial leverage to change the landscape of already exploited communities. Henry Meiggs, who was a railroad builder, had spent time building railroads across South American countries throughout the 1850s–70s, specifically in Chile and Peru to better facilitate these operations.

After building a railroad from Lima, Peru, to the Altiplano in the 1860s, Meiggs became known as 'Don Enrique'. Supposedly for his style of dictatorship over his operations. Meiggs was also known for having over a million dollars in debt with his ventures for business opportunities in other countries leaving said countries worse off than when he came. His son, Minor Cooper Keith, carried on the tradition and constructed a railroad to a port in Limon, Costa Rica, which would transport products, like bananas, to America. He was noted as the first man to take bananas to Southern America[10]. Having struck a deal with the Costa Rican President, Próspero Fernández Oreamuno, the railroad was built at no financial cost but incidentally cost the lives of over 5,000 men when a rockslide destroyed the tracks, taking the workers with it. [11]

Nevertheless, Cooper Keith's marketing of bananas allowed him to go and become one of the richest men in Costa Rica, marrying the president's daughter and tossing gold coins to Costa Rican children at the dockside when departing for sea voyages.[12] With the precedent of using intense labour and spinning governments in order to make big profits set it stone. It was only a matter of time before Andrew Preston of the Boston Fruit Company (a company operating in the same context as Cooper Keith, only in the Caribbean) went toe-to-toe with Keith for the American banana market. As it happens though, Keith and Preston decided to unite their resources of exploitation to become an even bigger powerhouse across both regions. Keith, who had come into financial turmoil at the time of a new deal[13], would go on to build railroads all over the South American regions, from Panama, Guatemala, Honduras to Nicaragua, Colombia and Ecuador[14], and Preston would go on to work aggressively to dominate the US market. Thus, the United Fruit Company was born.

The influence of the United Fruit Company grew to such heights that the *Los Angeles Times* once described Latin America as 'Uncle Sam's New Fruit Garden'.[15] This was an important description because it was Uncle Sam and his military squadron who killed banana workers after they went on strike against work conditions in Panama, Colombia and Guatemala.[16] Even the U.S Secret Service were enlisted to monitor Sam Zemurray, who became the president of the United Fruit Company in 1938. Before then, he was running his own banana operations in Honduras under the name Cuyamel Fruit Company.

Zemurray's operations were so influential in Honduras that he would find himself entangled between the US government, the British government and powerhouse company JP Morgan. When Honduras' tax debt to Britain kept increasing to unmanageable amounts in the early years of the 1900s, the American government, along with JP Morgan wanted to buy out the taxes in order to protect their interests and influence in the country. Zemurray saw this as bad news for his Cuyamel Fruit Company, who had been growing and had active operations in the country. So what did he do? As a lowly banana trader against a world major financial company and the American government? He rallied a few mercenaries and staged a coup, overthrowing the Honduran government and seizing even more control over the country.[17] As a result, the United Fruits Company decided the best way out of their predicament was to buy Cuyamel and make Zemurray the president of the company. This move would go on to change the landscape for American presence in Southern America for years to come.

I hope you're still with me. The United Fruit Company's presence in South America led to what people in the West understood as economic prosperity in the region. With new seaports and railroads being developed. Due to the devastating impacts of civil war between tribes in South and Central America and the Spanish-American War that ended just a year before the United Fruit Company emerged, many in the West saw the United Fruit Company as a tool for improvement and stabilization in the region. This belief was so widely held that even the *New York Times* referred to the reign of the company as the 'pinnacle of human achievement'.[18]

Of course, only a nation with such a questionable hand in foreign diplomacy would see the reign of the United Fruit Company as a good thing. The reality of the United Fruit Company's impact, as one might suspect, was far more problematic than many Westerners believed. The economies of the South and Central American countries that the company dominated were almost entirely reliant on exports to the U.S and Europe. Dramatically weakening domestic trade. The development of these countries was only in the interest of the profit attained and not the socio-economic development of their own communities. The intense and often violent level of labour demanded of South American workers threatened the life expectancy of industry workers, who did not have the opportunity to opt into different viable career paths. The conditions were so unbearable that workers in Colombia in 1928 attempted to stop working in protest, an action that would eventually lead to what was dubbed the 'banana massacres', an event that saw thousands of workers killed by guns hired by the United Fruits Company.

In response to the actions of the United Fruit Company, a rise in liberal and socialist thought led activists to spur 30,000 workers to go on strike in the same year of the massacre.[19] The response of the United Fruit Company was to hold the Colombian government hostage by implying that if things got worse, the U.S military would have to get involved to protect America's interest. The government conceded and deployed the Colombian military, killing over a thousand strikers.

The conditions for totalitarian rule were set in stone and it is impossible to really look at United Fruit Company and the rise of the banana market in America without seeing the bloody underbelly of it all.

Today, banana workers are supposedly better protected by fair trade standards and the United Fruits Company has gone on to reform and rebrand under the name Chiquita, a new fair trade brand.

But we haven't gotten too far from our issues yet. Just as cheap fruit meant cheap labour back then, today, the low price of Plantains and bananas means that cheap labour is still a present-day issue.

In 2013, Oliver Balch wrote a piece for *The Guardian* about the sustainability of bananas in the UK, quoted as the 'race to the bottom'.[20] Referring to retailers competing with each other to achieve the lowest prices for bananas and Plantains.

Under pressure from aggressive pricing policies, smaller producers are left with no options but to take what's given. Which more often than not is less than what they need to survive, let alone flourish.

In a study commissioned by the Make Fruit Fair campaign in 2015. A breakdown of Banana value chains for countries supplying to the EU showed that while retailers were enjoying 41% of the total value of the industry, workers were at the bottom of the totem pole with a small 7% value share and producers sharing 13.1% of the value.

In the same *Guardian* article, Balch remarks on the feelings of Alistair Smith about the wider socioeconomic and cultural impacts of such economic activity. Smith, the international coordinator of Banana Link, an organisation committed to fair and equitable production and trade in bananas, expressed that:

'The big losers in this battle are banana growers and their workers, most of whom are in poor countries in the Caribbean, South and Central America, and Africa. For farmers in former British colonies such as the Windward Islands, today's lower prices are compounding the effects of gradual trade deregulation, which has opened the European market to large-scale Latin American producers over recent years'.[21]

One of the largest Latin American producers is Chiquita, which already has a murky history with their large-scale production in the region. With the mention of 'gradual trade deregulation', it's easy to assume the concerns workers in the region would have. To further paint the picture of how trade deregulation can go wrong, in 2007, Chiquita were fined $25 million by US courts after admitting to paying roughly $1.7 million between 1994-2004 to the right-wing paramilitary group United Self-Defense Forces of Colombia, the AUC (Autodefensas Unidas de Colombia). Known as an organisation of death squads reportedly responsible for massacres, kidnappings and extortions.

Chiquita was suspected to have paid the AUC to help

'protect' their workers from other dangerous groups like FARC, The Revolutionary Armed Forces of Colombia— People's Army. However, in 2011, 4,000 Colombians accused Chiquita of being responsible for supporting the paramilitary who killed and tortured their relatives. In the early days of the United Fruit Company, Chiquita's former brand, built a railroad across Costa Rica in 1871 that Rich Cohen, author of *The Fish That Ate the Whale*, a book about Sam Zemurray, says potentially killed 4,000 people in laying the first 20 miles of the railroad.[22]

The US courts denied that Chiquita was directly responsible and the Colombian plaintiffs lost their case. The main US Chiquita company has long since disbanded its affiliations with any operations in Colombia, where other multinational companies like Uniban have started to take precedence.

Today working conditions in the banana and Plantain industry still leave a lot to be desired. Women make up less than a fifth of the global workforce[23] and without well enforced labour rules, deregulated operations allow for women to work at the risk of losing their jobs and benefits if they become pregnant. This is on top of a gender pay gap and the fact that a lot of women are denied opportunities to work in the more technically challenging or physically demanding jobs, which are generally better paid. Roles for women in the banana and Plantain export industry are usually reserved for packhouses, where women tend to receive lower wages.[24]

While these South American countries have a lot more to credit to their national problems than just the banana industry, it is an example of how big, corrupt banana and Plantain operations can have and have had a detrimental socio-cultural impact on working class communities putting at risk their health, finances and, in the saddest of cases, their lives.

Agriculture failings through government policies or lack thereof is yet another thing that works against the development of Plantains and bananas alike.

Kenneth Kobani, a produce grower from Rivers State, Nigeria, in conversation with *The Guardian Nigeria* cited the lack of Nigeria's government interventionist programmes as a major issue in the agricultural industry as a whole, including the Plantain sector.[25]

In 2014, Iyabo Adeoye of Nigeria's National Horticultural Research Institute and Oni Omobowale, a professor from the University of Ibadan, Department of Agricultural Economics stated that Nigeria's Plantain production 'is characterized by low usage of agricultural inputs, low mechanization and irrigation intensity. This is due to Nigeria's low investment in agriculture averaging approximately 2% of government expenditure'.[26]

In another instance, a Plantain farmer also based in Nigeria stated: 'To actualise the prospects of this [Plantain] crop... the country needs to grow more and add value through industrialisation'[27], going on to say: 'This will create jobs, reduce poverty and create wealth for the nation.'[28]

Similar sentiments were shared across Ghana. In 2015, before Nana Akufo-Addo became Ghana's fifth president, the country faced a dilemma. Through the mismanagement of government spending and subsidizing an overgrown civil service, Ghana racked up serious debt and turned to the

International Monetary Fund (IMF) for a $918 million bail-out.[29] With such a development occurring during his tenure, John Mahama, the then president of Ghana, was, in my own words, dun out ere*. When the time came for election campaigns in 2016, Nana Akufo-Addo attacked John Mahama's mismanagement of the agricultural industry, centering, of course, Plantain as a key indicator.

In Paris, May 2016, in a meeting for the New Patriotic Party, Nanu Akufo-Addo (its leader) and the then president of Ghana, John Mahama, Akufo-Addo spoke on Ghana's lack of Plantain production. Explaining that while neighbouring countries, like the Ivory Coast, were making strides, Ghana, under the leadership of President Mahama, was not. Akufo-Addo mentioned how under former President John Kofi Agyekum Kufuor, who left office in 2008, the total food import bill for the country, including Plantains, was $600 milion. Under another Ghanian president, John Dramani Mahama, who lost to Akufo-Addo in 2017, the bill rose to $1.5 billion. Akufo-Addo ended his speech by ironically saying: 'We are now importing Plantain into Ghana!'[30]

Which sounds ridiculous for a country that sits as one of the top 5 Plantain producing countries in the world. A closer look at the data shows that throughout Mahama's presidency, Ghana's Plantain production was actually operating at a trade surplus, meaning they were still making and producing more Plantain and bananas than they were importing from neighbouring countries. A trade surplus, meaning positive relationship between income and cost, usually reflects on the country's GDP (Gross Domestic Products). When GDP, the total value goods and services produced in an economy, rises it likely means that jobs are being created and the economy is growing. Sounds good, but to Akufo-Addo's point, things were

---

*   Finished

starting to look a bit leaveit* as time went on.

In 2012, around the beginning of Mahama's administration, the imports of bananas and Plantains, fresh and dried, were valued at $217,096 for the year. Far less than the value of exports valued at $1,859,219, which was a trade surplus of over 750%. Towards the end of Mahama's administration in January 2017, the country's Plantains' and bananas' productions were still operating at a surplus. Despite the value of exports going down in value from $1,859,219 to $1,540,628 and so on. The value of imports only ever went up, from $217,096 in 2012, $352,404 in 2016 to $380,226 in 2017 until they started dropping again during Akufo-Addo's administration.[31]

These statistics never threatened Ghana's trade surplus with the banana and Plantain industry, but they do show a pattern that gave Akufo-Addo enough ammo for his campaign.

To remedy this, in the wake of Nana Akufo-Addo's election win in 2017, his party, NPP, introduced the Planting for Food and Jobs (PFJ) policy.[32] Launched in 2017, the policy had three main goals: to modernize the agricultural sector of the economy, create employment and reduce poverty. In the same instance, the government had approved $200,000 for the construction of a Plantain-processing factory focused on processing Plantain flour and other by-products of the fruit for local consumption, exports and job creation.

It's worth noting that exports for bananas and Plantains in Ghana rose from 2017 to 2018 (Akufo-Addo's first year of presidency) where they went from $30,971,362 to $46,709,107 while imports decreased from $380,226 to $303,659 and to $22,096 in 2019,[33] correlating with Akufo-Addo's plan for the industry.

---

* A slang term popularised by Lethal Bizzle, meaning a thing or individual is better left alone due to its poor quality or lack of value.

No amount of quantitative data can provide complete insight into the livelihood of an industry. For one, a rise in exports does not reflect the quality of an industry entirely. It doesn't account for things like: how a workforce is treated or wider socio-economic impacts. However, what the data does provide is an insight into when a government ignores its agricultural development versus when it invests in it.

PLANTAIN, PESTICIDES AND BANANAS

Chemicals have been used to kill off pests for thousands of years. The earliest recorded deliberate use of pesticide can be traced to 2500 BC, when the Sumerians rubbed smelly sulfur into their skin in the hope of repelling mites and insects.[34]

In a study done in 2011 by the Central American Institute for Studies on Toxic Substances in Costa Rica, it was found that the majority of indigenous Plantain farmers had 'some general knowledge of pesticides concerning crop protection but little on acute health effects and hardly any on exposure routes and pathways and chronic effects.'[35] On transnational company plantations, workers reported that they felt safe and protected using 'formalized' practices; however, workers in smallholders, which are small-scale farms, reported that pesticide handling was not even perceived as hazardous and as a result no safety precautions were recognized or applied.[36]

So, what is a pesticide exactly? Well, a pesticide is basically any substance or mixture of substances, usually chemical compositions, that are used to prevent, destroy, repel or mitigate the invasion of pests on crops in agriculture.[37] They are used widely for pest control in most agricultural operations.

Exposure to pesticides can cause a number of health effects and are linked to a range of serious illnesses and diseases, from respiratory problems to cancer.[38]

During WWII, when the need to produce more food became urgent, an increase in synthetic pesticides such as aldrin, DDT, parathion and others were developed to help respond quickly to food shortages.[39] In 1962, Rachel Carson, a marine biologist from America, published *Silent Spring*, a book that laid out the problems that haphazard use of pesticides could have on human health and the environment. The book, supported by the JFK administration, led to a rise in consciousness about pesticide dangers and was the catalyst behind the discontinuation of chemicals like Dichlorodiphenyltrichloroethane (DDT).[40]

As years went by, safer and systematically used pesticides have been developed and applied to agricultural processes, but not without great risk including, but not limited to, things like air pollution, contamination of water bodies, killing aquatic life and threatening wildlife, which in turn damages ecosystems. In 2018, a study done by the University of Guelph in Ontario, Canada, showed that low-level exposure to pesticides mirrors the cell mutations that cause Parkinson's disease.[41]

Pesticides and agrochemicals are particularly a risk to women who work with these chemicals. In part of a global report done by Anna Cooper for Banana Link in 2015, research in Latin American regions found, 'some women had vomited blood and were provided with no medical assistance from the company'[42], and in another instance, 'one sprayer had a miscarriage several months into her pregnancy even though she did not spray whilst pregnant.'[43] Even though a lot of smaller producers enlist third parties to perform manual spraying, in uncontrolled environments it's not uncommon for nearby people to be exposed.

In the same global report, Anna quotes how in 2014 the Regional Institute on Toxic Substances of Costa Rica's National University (Instituto Regional en Sustancias Tóxicas de la Universidad Nacional, IRET-UNA) found high levels of Ethylene Thiourea (ETU) in the urine of women living near banana-producing regions in the Limón province in Costa Rica. ETU has been known to cause dizziness, sweating, nausea, increased heart rate and blood pressure with exposure. This specific report found that the women had levels of ETU that exceeded the safe level established by the US Environmental Protection Agency's Integrated Risk Information System.

ISSA DISEASE EPIDEMIC

As we have seen so far there are many opps* working against the prosperity and success of Plantain and banana growth. However, there is one particular problem that might take home the prize for being the biggest pain in the inflorescence. It is the agricultural industry's equivalent of Limewire's infamous, 'I did not have sexual relations with that woman' bug (if you don't understand the reference, just move on).

Viruses and diseases.

With a list of different types of diseases extending to over 50. Bacterial and fungal diseases have been the cause of destruction for entire fields of banana and Plantain crops, halting operations on a mass scale since forever. In the earlier days of big banana companies, the transportation of bananas, and less so Plantains, were via the sea where they would be

---

*   The opposition or enemies.

stored in large bulk containers. At the time this was an effective means of the crop's transportation because everything was timed perfectly.

And by timed perfectly, I refer to the organised timing of the planting, the yielding, the picking, the cutting, the ripening, the packing, the loading, the shipping, the loading, the unloading and the store placement that was all done in perfect time. The entire operation for banana companies worked like clockwork. Until it didn't.

Cue the violins...

Because whilst everything was going seemingly swimmingly for the banana market, good old mother nature came to ruin profit margins just because she can.

Infectious organisms like fungi, bacteria and viruses came to ruin the day. Diseases like the Fusarium wilt, better known as the Panama disease, have the ability to infect bananas so vigorously that it can turn entire hectares of promising yield to fields of zombie leaves. This is actually what happened to the world's former favourite banana. The Gros Michel banana, which was the Beyoncé of the Banana family before its reign came to a crashing end, came to blows with the unforgiving Panama disease and lost.

Before going extinct in the 1950s, the Gros Michel banana was the number one ranked banana cultivar in the world. It was understood to be tastier, more resistant to bruising, better suited for shipping and it was easily propagated. The Gros Michel was agriculturally cloned throughout plantations far and wide. From the early 1830s, all the way through to its extinction, the demand for the banana perpetually skyrocketed. The United Fruit Company ensured they could supply the fruit and, in turn, they would start a process known as 'monoculture', which would ultimately lead to the demise of the overseas consumption of the Gros Michel forever.

Monoculture is the cultivation of a single crop in any given area. Taking your best, biggest seller and using the largest land you have available to multiply it. The system works because the growing, maintenance and general production processes can develop as standard, making for an easier, more familiar production process, eliminating the risks of imperfections since every crop is a clone of itself.

As far as the United Fruit Company was concerned, monoculture was making sense and making cents. Millions of them. Then, in 1997,[44] the bananapocalypse happened. Banana plantations across Australia started to pop up with dead crops. Like a scene out of *Stranger Things*, leaves were wilted, soil became contaminated and growers were forced to completely abandon entire plantation fields. Sure enough, with international trade at such a high and everyone producing the same crop, everybody's plantations were a target. Left, right and centre, banana plants were toppling and markets were dying. This was the Panama disease.

The Panama disease was a fungus spread by way of contaminated soil whereby a minute of exposed soil could carry the wilt to a new plantation where it could, and did, last for decades and the horror of it all, was that it was completely immune to chemical treatments.[45] This kind of story isn't in any way new to agriculture either. The biggest lesson learned, or at least should have been learned, was from the Irish potato famine that taught us, when you plan your entire agricultural operation around the cultivation of a single crop, a killer bacteria can come to take your livelihood, with no questions asked and you will be f@!'d.

A potato variety known as the Irish Lumper was the main food source for the majority of working-class Irish folk in the mid 1800s. When the Phytophthora infestans, a micronism that caused the late blight disease, came to Ireland, it took with it the life of almost all the Irish Lumpers at the time. The detrimental impact of this disease resulted in at least a year's worth of crops depleted and causing the death of almost one million people due to starvation. The Irish population was recorded to have fallen by 50% with a number of nationals desperately emigrating to America and other parts of Europe.[46] As a major event in the nation's history, the famine went on to inspire a conclusive change to Ireland's political and socio-cultural landscape.[47]

In a similar fashion, as a result of the Panama disease, the Gros Michel was completely annihilated. Luckily, today the Cavendish banana and Horn Plantain, which make up 99% of the banana varieties eaten in the Western world today, are okay.

But with all these tales of farming debacles, you'd be forgiven for thinking companies would disband the use of an agricultural system that was so vulnerable. But with a number of single crop markets still dominating and the amount of £££ that there is to be made, the threat of diseases and terrible histories, hasn't been enough to strike any fear.

As the ghosts of the Gros Michel wail over the plantations they once ruled, new and improved variations of the Panama disease have been lurking in plantations across the globe. Like most other diseases and viruses, the Panama disease has different varieties that present new dangers. The first instance of the Panama disease that got rid of the Gros Michel was known as 'Race 1'. Interestingly, Race 1 couldn't destroy the newer Cavendish banana or any of the Plantain varieties.

However, slowly lurking and plotting on our farm lands is a new strain of the Panama disease. One that has come with the tenacity and the energy of Lil Jon adlib. This newer strain of the Panama disease has been dubbed 'the Tropical Race 4' (TR4), and it has been reported to pose a threat to 80%

of the world's varieties in cultivation in 2014 including the Cavendish banana.[48]

Currently, there isn't enough evidence to prove that Plantain is as susceptible to TR4.[49] But the deadliness of the Panama disease lies in the fact that unlike other Plantain and banana diseases, the Panama disease cannot be killed by chemicals or agricultural ingenuity. And while there isn't enough evidence to prove that Plantain is as susceptible to TR4,[50] the disease's ever changing and developmental nature means the threat to other Musa species, including Plantains, is always looming.

The Panama disease is believed to have its hunting grounds in Malaysia, where journalist Gwynn Guilford described its presence as a, 'bloodsport between Panama disease and wild bananas.'[51] What Guildford meant by this is that while we were all enjoying bananas and Plantains willy nilly, somewhere in Malaysia, the Panama disease that attacked bananas met its match with the wild banana.

The story goes that when the disease tried to kill off the wild bananas, the bananas, through stages of natural selection, actually became stronger and in turn were able to develop resistance to the disease. However, this process provoked the disease, which in turn, also became stronger.

When production of Plantains and bananas moved to and from Asia and Latin America, the Panama disease hopped on board, facing the Gros Michel banana, which had no capacity for resistance.[52] It is generally understood that the movement towards global production is what accelerated the spread of the Panama disease. Exporters hungry for big produce numbers have taken the production of bananas and Plantains beyond their natural habitat giving the Panama disease free reign to roam and destroy.[53]

With all these criticisms of the Plantain and banana industry, observers are wondering, what is next to come for this deeply complex industry? What will the next big development in the Plantain and banana world be? Herein enters the subject of genetic modification, also known as GMO. Some botanical scientists believe that GMO will become the next hot topic in the banana and Plantain world.

As previously mentioned, the Musa species which houses Plantains and bananas, is no stranger to a bit of DNA remixing. The fruits have already gone through genetic refinement for the benefit of human consumption, albeit naturally cultivated. Genetic modification is defined as a change in the characteristics of a plant, animal or micro-organism by transferring a piece of DNA from one organism to a different organism. The assumption many make about GMO is that it is engineered via man-made mechanisms, which is not true. Fruits and vegetables can be naturally genetically modified too.

The case for man-made GMO Plantains and bananas is that the fruits are able to be engineered to resist diseases and other oogly booglies. On top of the resistance to disease, genetically modified bananas and Plantains could introduce other key benefits such as reducing food waste, as they could be made to ripen slower.

Plantain and bananas are a main source of nutrition for entire communities in countries like Uganda, Rwanda and Cameroon where consumption of Plantain and bananas collectively reached over 200 kg per capita in 2018.[54] Welcoming another benefit of genetically modified Plantains and bananas is the potential for additional nutrition much like how genetically modified rice known as 'Golden Rice' was created with a better intake of vitamin A.[55]

However, the hysteria around anything GMO seems to be too much for the market to embrace. Concerns around the prospect of the man-made perfect banana are wide, varied and in a sense, justified. The worries range from allergies all the way to organ damage.

As early as 1988, the Honduran Agricultural Research Foundation (FHIA) created the FHIA-01. It sounds like a *Dragonball Z* android, I know, but the FHIA-01 is actually a synthetic hybrid banana marketed under the name 'Goldfinger'.[56] The FHIA-01 is a synthetic banana and a noteworthy one as it was developed using selective breeding programmes to be resistant to the Panama disease and the Black sigatoka disease. The FHIA-01 represents a success of genetic engineering. The breeding programme takes advantage of chromosome maths. Tetraploids, which are plants with four copies each of chromosomes (XXXX), get crossed with a diploid (XX) to make triploids (XXX).

Tetraploids (XXXX) + Diploid (XX) = Triploids (XXX)

As explained in previous chapters, triploid plants can't produce their own seeds and bear seedless fruits. To the same effect, triploids can cross with diploids to make triploids. Using the right parents, a hybrid can be born with new genetic qualities. The only real issue with the FHIA-01 is that it isn't a Cavendish banana and therefore hasn't had the same amount of global marketing needed to properly enter wider markets. The development of better hybrids of Plantain have also been a feature in some agricultural movements, particularly in Africa where most of the world's Plantain production takes place.

The International Institute of Tropical Agriculture (IITA) in Nigeria has won awards for their breeding programme, which, over the past 30 years has been developing better Plantain hybrids.[57] In 2019, an article was published by CORAF, an international non-profit association of national agricultural research systems in over 23 West and Central African countries.[58] They credited the IITA for 'Plantain cultivation in Burkina Faso,' which was rare at the time.[59]

According to a study titled 'Promising High-Yielding Tetraploid Plantain-Bred Hybrids in West Africa', farmers growing Plantain hybrids, bred more often due to the Plantains' resistance to things like pests and pathogens.[60] One of the hybrid Plantains created resulted in a Plantain that is even resistant to the disease black sigatoka.[61]

Would you care for a GMO Plantain?

COOPERATIVES & FAIRTRADE

Amidst all these layers of complications in the Musa industry, one consistent facet is the struggles of farmers, producers and growers in Africa, Latin America and the Caribbean. Life for small producers in the industry hasn't been the easiest. The damage of big companies behaving like trapstars has meant that getting by, for many producers, growers and their workers has at times been unfeasible. Perhaps no story of the banana related struggle rings as true as it does for the communities of Plantain and banana growers in the Latin American 'Banana Republics'. These nations have had to recover from decades of what was effectively neo-colonialism at the hands of the United Fruit Company alongside the fact that many work environments in the Plantain and banana industry were deregulated. Thus, the only way to reverse the effects of such a damaging trade was to do it themselves, in ways that work for their communities.

Such is the story of Coobana. Coobana was created in 1991 by a group of workers who felt hard done by the industry. Located in Changuinola in the district of Panama, the organisation was initially started by 74 workers.[62] The aim of Coobana was to empower the worker community with a trade that values their efforts. That meant no more dodgy work conditions, low wages and neglect. After the initial struggles of setting up Coobana, including the fluctuations of banana prices and the cost of production, their loan for the land was paid off.

Coobana became Fairtrade certified in 2010 and they were able to negotiate a trade deal with a buyer in the UK, shipping from a port in Costa Rica. With hectares of lands ruined from deserted monoculture production, Coobana have funded and managed a reforestation programme, environmental education programmes and have even seen through a sea turtle monitoring programme. All of which would not have made any sense for companies whose priorities were cheaper and cheaper costs of production.

The wider industry's obsession with attaining cheap costs has been the impetus behind many other organisations that seek to protect the communities central to banana and Plantain production. Coobana is just one. Others include COLSIBA (Coordinating Unions in Latin America) that work to include specific details on protecting women in the industry,[63] to groups like SINUTRABE, an Ecuadorian plantation workers' union that delivered Covid-19 relief packages to communities in the country amidst government cuts in 2020.[64]

Similar movements have also developed in Africa. From Fako Agricultural Workers Union (FAWU) in Cameroon that have promoted better working conditions, wages, education, labour rights, women's rights and have also participated in trade union meetings with companies from the Ivory Coast, Ghana and within Cameroon, bridging francophone-anglophone relations.[65]

The General Agricultural Workers' Union of Ghana (GAWU) have also been a driving force for Plantain and banana communities as the biggest trade union for farmers and agricultural employees in Ghana.

The happenings of all these groups seem to be underpinned by a development in the agricultural industry that has become a huge force in the industry. A development known as fair trade. The concept of fair trade is quite simple. It is trade between producers and nations where producers, namely farmers and workers are paid fairly. It is there to empower workers and farmers, giving them more say in their working life.

Fair trade's earliest traces, according to the World Fair Trade Organization, date back to 1946 in Puerto Rico, but when considering how long international trade has existed, fair trade is a fairly new concept. Championed by Christain Aid, Oxfam, Traidcraft, the World Development Movement and the National Federation of Women's Institutes, the Fairtrade Foundation was established in 1992. It then developed into Fairtrade International in 1997.

The average person is most familiar with Fairtrade through its epochal label, associated 'good trade' world wide, a label that can be found plastered on your packets of fruits and vegetables.

Fairtrade labels first appeared on products in 1997, and they tell us that a product has been produced in accordance with fair trade standards, which include things like workers' rights. In most cases, a Fairtrade label also means the company selling the products will have paid a marked-up price for goods that go towards helping producers from poorer countries.[66]

The extra money is often used for the development of schools, hospitals, production scale ups, etc. Groups like Coobana, which became Fairtrade certified in 2010 after forming in 1991, reference fair trade as a necessary feature to their cooperative's development. In one of Banana Link's videos covering Coobana, a worker named Mateo Santo referenced being able to buy a larger space for his family to live after access to fair trade due to a grant paid to 200 workers to improve their living conditions, subsidised by the Fairtrade Premium.[67] In 2019, Fairtrade released their 'Monitoring the Scope and Benefits of Fairtrade Bananas 10th edition report', that covered 173 banana producers and 25,000 farmers in 18 countries. The report concluded that €31.3 million was paid to banana producers for the year. The report goes on to give a range of data representing how fair trade movements have impacted banana production, covering countries like the Dominican Republic, Colombia, Mexico and more. Interestingly, as extensive as the report was there was no mention of Plantain.[68]

Searching 'Plantain' on Fairtrade's website gave me a maximum of maybe six results and not in a particularly insightful way either. This pales in comparison to the search for 'banana', which gave me 300 results covering a wide range of issues with banana production centered in each piece.

I tried to find some information on Fairtrade Plantain but I couldn't find anything. This tells me one of two things. **1)** They don't exist, or **2)** we are inclined to assume that whatever positive developments take place in the banana world, must, *fingers crossed*, take place in the world of Plantain. So, I cannot categorically give you an answer for where all the Fairtrade Plantains are.

In an article Alicia Kennedy wrote for *Vice*, she quotes Jessica Jones-Hughes and Ann Brown, representative of Fairtrade America, saying that Europe has a bigger demand for fair trade items, but the only fair trade Plantains Brown had heard of were Plantain chips called Zamora Plantain Crisps from Ecuador that are sold in the UK and France.[69]

Zamora Plantain Crisps became the first Fairtrade crisps sold in the UK. Based in Edinburgh, selling naturally sweet and spicy flavours, Zamora Plantain Crisps won the Great Taste Award in 2013.

It is important to understand that there are many companies operating on fair terms without actually being registered with Fairtrade because no organisation is not without its criticisms. Amidst the ongoing Haitian-Dominican Republic migration issue, where groups of Haitians in DR have been forced to leave the country due to growing tensions in Haitian-DR relations, Luciano Robles, representative of the Trade Union Autonomous Federation, commented on Fairtrade standards simply not doing enough to help the migrant workers back in 2012.[70]

Another criticism of the Fairtrade model is that it doesn't mitigate more competitive pricing undercutting total sales for produce. In an article in *The Guardian* by Ndongo Samba Sylla, he cites how 'only 28% of Fairtrade coffee was sold in Fairtrade markets. Fairtrade bananas are the best selling product (56%-64%), while Fairtrade tea is the least selling product (7%).'[71] Supply is higher than demand for all Fairtrade products, which would inevitably lead to lower prices with producers struggling to compete.

In another criticism of the fair trade system by Sylla, he states: 'Fairtrade-certified articles tend to be based on products usually exported by Latin American countries,[72] and as a result, Latin American countries doubly benefit in comparison to African and Asian countries.'

Sylla goes on to explain that if the fair trade system had been 'born in an African context,' it would concentrate on mining industries and petroleum production. In the case of Plantain, Africa is also the biggest producer. A lack of fair trade coverage on Plantain is arguably representative of the lack of coverage and inclusion of Africa in this arena.

Whilst there is some confusion around whether Fairtrade is really as effective as it claims to be, there is one important impact of it that is worth noting: the development of Fairtrade has inspired consumers to ask more important questions about the food they buy and eat. Consumers are now more conscious about where their food comes from, if it was produced sustainably, if the producers are treated fairly and all that jazz.

So while it could be some time before we see Fairtrade Plantains, it doesn't hurt to open the dialogue. For the Black diaspora in the UK, Plantain problems are really our problems.

PLANTAIN INFLATION

With all this talk about global events , it might be about time to come home. Where the only worry of most of the British Plantainers is the increasing cost of God's favourite fruit. For the longest time, Plantainers of my generation were used to seeing a £1 coin and knowing that it was equivalent to 3 maybe 4 well ripened Plantains. Just like £1 was never really £1 in secondary school, but at least 6 wings, and a drink for an extra 50p.

In the early days of school ties and blazers, most of us would usually start the day with £1.50 or £2 and we were sitting on a surplus. Any more than that, and we'd have to question your socioeconomic background. We knew the value of £1. And we couldn't imagine a day that bossman* would

---

*   A term popularised by young people to refer to shopkeepers in local convenient stores or fast food takeaways.

ever ask for more money. You can then imagine what it was like for hundreds of Black Brits growing up in an era that started to see that £1 for 3 Plantains was a thing of the past. £1.20, £1.50, and £1 for 2? idonbelieveit! It may have been no more than an extra £1 or a 20p, but that was enough to rock our world and shake our cores. So much so, it led to brief psychogenic tremors amongst the Black British community.

In 2017, my friend Lex Amor tweeted that she, 'Purchased Plantain at a rate of 2 for £1 today out of sheer desperation. My hands are still trembling'. Two years later *@RonkeLawal* tweeted that MP Chuku Umunna's political campaign focused on more important things, like Plantain inflation.[73]

Seventy-eight per cent of the people who took my Plantain survey said they'd seen an increase in the price of the fruit. Since people started noticing the rise in price, they have also wanted to know what was causing it. Were Plantain extracts being slapped in boujee skin care products? Was England pressuring us out? Was this 'go back to your country' but hidden in inflated prices? Maybe it was Brexit? Everybody needed answers. While some people settled for believing this was what happened due to food gentrification. Others saw the potential correlation between Brexit trade deals and a weakening pound. A safe bet considering most of us treat Plantain as an inelastic good.*

So what is the truth? Well there is one possible answer, but it isn't a nice one. And that is, the cost of Plantain production is rising, reflected in its increased pricing. Basic supply and demand laws tell us that when the supply of a product

---

* An inelastic good is an economic term referring to the static quantity of a good or service when its price changes. Inelastic meaning that when the price goes up, consumers' buying habits/demand stay about the same, and when the price goes down, consumers' buying habits/demand also remain unchanged. As opposed to an elastic where the demand for a product increases/decreases a lot when the price changes.

decreases, the demand and the price will do the opposite. Especially when a product is inelastic.

As we've explored the problems with Plantain and banana production around the world, we now understand the livelihood of Plantains is being held in the balance due to threats coming from everywhere. Plant diseases causing rocky stabilities within the industry are one of the biggest threats yet. While the latest strain of the Panama disease hasn't yet proven to be as big a danger to Plantain as it is to the Cavendish banana, who really knows if a Plantain-killing disease is in the wake?

Plantain producers also face threats from other nasty actors. The banana bunchy top virus, black sigatoka and weevils to name a few. Black sigatoka, in particular, has been known to wipe out 50% yield. To address these issues, more Plantain producers, particularly of the smaller varieties, will need, with a move towards formalising the industry, to invest in more and better quality fertilizers, fossil fuels and pesticides.

There is also a possibility that the industry resorts to reversing the effects of monoculture—using polyculture and agroforestry, which, unlike the aforementioned monoculture, is an approach to agriculture where farmers grow more than one species on the same land in the hopes of imitating the diversity of natural ecosystems. This process is in turn meant to lead to a more sustainable form of agriculture. It will take time, effort and most importantly resources. The transition for many producers would rely on financial injections, from Fairtrade Premiums, government investment, higher prices and all the above.

The unforgiving effects of climate change are yet another threat to the supply of Plantain. Drastic changes in weather have made it more difficult for producers to guarantee meeting demand in a profession that was already vulnerable to pre-climate change weather.

In 2019, *Fresh Plaza*, a global trade media platform covering news from the fresh produce industry, posted a story on their website covering the droughts and tornadoes in the Dominican Republic that had impacted Plantain production. They cited that, in some cases, the price of Plantain had jumped as high as 50% following the loss of yields.[74] According to a study by Dan Bebber at the University of Essex, the impact of climate change threatens yearly reductions in Plantain and banana yields globally and by 2050 it could reverse all the positive developments of the industry with significant reductions.[75]

So, as sad as it is, the production of Plantain could really be in jeopardy. Trevon Fuller, lead researcher on a project that studied possible links between increased temperature changes and Plantain growth in Cameroon, observed a 43% decrease in Plantain production between 1991 and 2011. Fuller stated: 'Hotter temperatures are accompanied by increased dryness of the air, which places stress on plants during fruit development leading to lower yields.'[76]

In the last 20 years or so, most Black British folk, particularly from working-class backgrounds in London, have noticed the very visible changes to the socioeconomic-cultural landscape of their communities that have turned 'gentrification' into one of the dirtiest words in modern British vocabulary. Gentrification, as defined by Google, is the process of a poor area changing in favour of an affluent demographic moving into the area. This often takes the form of 'improved' housing, new businesses and folk with larger purses, attracting increased prices from local shops in the community, which in turn displaces the original inhabitants of said area.

In a city like London, many areas with a high population of working-class Black Afro-Caribbean communities have fallen victim to gentrification. Influxes of mostly young middle-class white people are attracted to these areas by cheap house prices and the inviting appeal of the 'ends'.

Gentrification also impacts the food economy of an area. Due to the influx of a new affluent demographic, retailers sell seemingly high-quality food that is deliberately priced at a higher price for the newer demographic in the area. It's within this context that a lot of people assert food gentrification as one of the main causes for the price inflation of Plantain. The term 'food gentrification' gets thrown around a lot and while there is not an agreed consensus on its definition, it is generally referenced when foods traditionally consumed by ethnic minorities and/working-class communities are 'discovered' by outside communities as new, hip and exciting foods. In the short run, these rapid increases in demand push prices up before the supply of said food can respond. Ultimately pushing once accessible foods out of economic reach for the communities who have always eaten them.

All in all. It seems you can flip a coin and choose the answer you desire for the price change of Plantain.

Have the systematic failures of an industry, from mono-crop exhaustion, resource mismanagement and the struggles of dealing with botanically poisoning opps caught up with all of us? Or is it that the gentrifiers have actually come over the hill armed with weapons of mass inflation? The choice you make really reflects on how you choose to see the food industry and the crux of its main issues. However you look at it though, there are layers behind what's pushing up Plantain prices and it is more than likely a combination of all the reasons mentioned.

Through observation of its history, the agricultural industry is nowhere near the perfectly peaceful and equitably trans-actional industry that marketing campaigns would like us to believe. The industry is drenched in blood, sweat and tears and not of the good variety. There's pain, there's injustice, there's neglect, there's criminality and a lot more.

The profit-oriented developments of an industry that became unmanageably global has led it deep into dark waters. In those waters, people have drowned and are drowning still under irresponsible practice. In the midst of it all, are you and I, the consumers wondering where do we go? What do we do? On most days, I still buy Plantain without knowing or feeling any different. In light of all these problems, buying and eating Plantain without any real hurdles is such a familiar process it's hard to imagine anything changing. But that's an attitude towards food consumption that seems to have an imminent expiry date. Daniel Bebber of the University of Exeter said: 'The story of the banana is really the story of modern agriculture exemplified in a single fruit... It has all of the ingredients of equitability and sustainability issues, disease pressure, and climate change impact all in one. It's a very good lesson for us.'[77]

For many of us, including me, we might learn the hard way.

PLANTAIN
WORD
COUNT:
851

7

PLANTAIN NOW AND IN THE FUTURE

Here's a fun fact about Plantain. This is now the seventh chapter of this book. Seven plus one equals eight. Eight rotated by a 180-degree angle transforms into the infinity sign.

Ergo, Plantain will last forever.

Well let's hope so anyway. Because to fry Plantain is life. To flip. To mash. To boil. To roast. To dice. To slice. To feast. To share. To hoard. To hold. To harvest. To grow. To have Plantain. Is everything you need sometimes.

I can't think back to a time when I was without Plantain and to be honest, I don't want to imagine a time when I was. Even when I'm old and grey. When my children have become old enough to question my authority. When the mistakes of my 20s are a drop in the ocean of my thoughts. I hold the hope that my kitchen, decorated with Kerry James Marshall pieces and J Hus wall quotes will house organic, ethically sourced and traded Plantains.

With my passion for Plantain fuelling the words you are reading now, you'd think the prospect of writing this book would have been easy for me. You'd think my fingers would never have left my keyboard. And, yes, when I shifted into gear, I was off. But in the beginning it was a struggle. When I first sat down with an empty page on Google docs, I thought to myself: 'Wait. What! I'm writing a book about Plantain?' *confused emoji*

In the early stages of trying to conceptualise what a book about Plantain could be, I was questioning whether I could really do it. What was there to say? What does a book on Plantain entail? How could I do the fruit that I love so much, justice? The more I asked those questions, the more fugazi it started to look each time I opened my laptop.

The blinking insertion point never seemed to move far from its starting space. I was stuck. Then, thankfully, the change came when a friend of mine, with a hint of sarcasm in his voice, asked me: 'how can you write a book about Plantain lol?' I could sense the subtle mockery in his tone, vibrating through the sonants. For some reason, coming out of his mouth, the same question I had been asking myself now sounded like pure ignorance. 'What do you mean, "how can I write a book about Plantain?" Are you stupid? Are you dumb?' And with that, the weights had been lifted off of my shoulders. I felt like the men in Snickers adverts that feel like themselves again when they've finally had a bite. At some point I went back and realised I had to chomp down on what Plantain is. So I could give it its much deserved respect and reverence the whole world should know about. Beyond a fruit, a berry and a cookable happy pill. What *is* Plantain? What is the story of Musa Paradisiaca that everyone should know?

When talking to Ifeyinwa, co-founder of Chuku's restaurant she told me, 'the thing is, I don't even need you to like it. I need you to respect it. This crop is levels. Respect it. If you enjoy it, that's a bonus, but Plantain's brilliance doesn't just come from its taste.'

Looking at the story of Plantain invites us to explore stories of many things. Botany. Triploids. Diploids. The many ups and downs in the world of agriculture. Viruses. Political scandals. Workers' rights. The movement of peoples. Global trade.

Neo-colonialism and more.

I realised that to explore Plantain meant to explore all these different things. I started to appreciate how much one could actually write. Plantain is a cultural artefact. A cultural artefact that continues to develop. For some of us, it can tell us stories of who we are, where we have been and who we have been. Knowing its journey throughout global histories, the hands its legacy has passed through, how could I not write a book about it?

Now I know my Plantain craze isn't a complete result of potential madness. Instead valid appreciation of a true culinary treasure.

Plantain is your great great great great-grandmother who hasn't yet aged and seems like she never will. She makes the best food. She tells you the best stories about her travels around the globe and she brings out the best of you. You can't explain why, but she does.

So where's my call to action? What do I need you to do with all this information? When it comes to food, particularly what's considered cultural foods, who is going to make sure these high streets we call our own, have what we need in 50 years? Who, if not us? Restaurants like Chuku's and many others ensure the foods we love are present, visible and accessible in the communities we call our own. The other day I was talking to my bro about moving out of London, and we ended up laughing. Because even with all the financial prospects of buying a house up north for £20, the thought of not being close to anywhere that stocks Plantain and other necessary Black foods is unimaginable.

Not too long ago, I asked one of the shopkeepers in my area why he didn't sell Plantain. He looked me in the face and said 'nobody wants.' Luckily. Out of the six corner stores located in my area I can count on two of them to have at least one trusty box of Plantains ready for me to take. But I can't help thinking, what if one day, the shopkeepers of those stores turn around and say, 'nobody wants' too. It's a scary reality I don't want to imagine it.

Of course, the prerequisites for nationwide administrations of Plantain takes a lot. It takes investment. Development of international trade relationships. Market spaces to infiltrate and years of dedication.

But if you've made it this far into this book. It's either because you're a supportive friend and I appreciate you. Or, like me, you want to see Plantain in your shops, in your eateries, and kitchens for the foreseeable future too. It's up to us to make sure that happens.

Slapping boxes of Plantain on supermarket shelves won't work either. The story of the quinoa crop and its 'discovery' in the West teaches how things can go wrong, when communities that relied on the crop as staple food were priced out of affording it.

So like all good things, it is about balance. We want the world to appreciate Plantain for the delicious and interesting fruit that it is. But we also want Plantain farmers, producers and local communities that rely on the fruit to benefit too. True Plantainers should want to understand the truth behind how Plantain arrives to them. The workings of the markets that bring it to us. As consumers, we are as attached to the growers and producers of Plantain as they are to us. Don't be surprised if in 2023, I start shottin boxes of Plantain from São Tomé outside your local high street.

Hopes, wishes and calls of action aside. Speaking to Christian Adofo, my fellow *A Quick Ting On* brother, he said something that stuck with me and illustrated something that I want to leave you with. I asked him what Plantain culture meant to him and he said, 'enjoyment. A prelude for people to relax around food which is nourishing and well-seasoned.' Because that's where my love for Plantain starts and that's where it ends. Enjoyment. For you and for me. Because none of

this would be worth it, if Plantain didn't, at least, give us that. And on that note, I end this love letter, with a statement that by now, we should all agree with. A reminder that Plantain is a one-of-a-kind fruit. That brings with it an array of histories, cultures and more. Stories of innovation. Hardship. Politics. Love and struggle. Most importantly though, one of the most well deserving sweetnesses on earth. Now go and enjoy it.

REFERENCES

CHAPTER 1: MY LIFE AND PLANTAIN

Lindsay-Prince, Lemara, et al. *Plantain Papers Issue 2*. 2019.

CHAPTER 2: THE HISTORY OF PLANTAIN

Bananas and Plantains, Origins, History and Differences. (2011, February 12). El Valle de Anton, Panama. El Valle the Volcanic Village. El Valle's History, Attractions and Information. https://elvalleinformation.wordpress.com/bananas-and-plantains/

Barkham, P. (1999, March 5). *The banana wars explained*. The banana wars explained. Retrieved 2020, from https://www.theguardian.com/world/1999/mar/05/eu.wto3

Blench, R. (2009). Bananas and Plantains in Africa: Re-interpreting the linguistic evidence. 363-380. https://core.ac.uk/download/pdf/5101777.pdf

Bryant, A. (2018, February 6). *Many Food Names in English Come From Africa*. Learning English Voa News. https://learningenglish.voanews.com/a/many-food-names-in-english-come-from-africa/4236534.html

CHAPTER 4: THE WAR OF PRONUNCIATION

Hadid, Diaa. "Pakistan Wants You To Know: Most Pink Himalayan Salt Doesn't Come From India." *Pakistan Wants You To Know: Most Pink Himalayan Salt Doesn't Come From*

India, 3 October 2019, https://www.npr.org/sections/thesalt/2019/10/03/763960436/pakistan-wants-you-to-know-most-pink-himalayan-salt-doesnt-come-from-india. Accessed 2020.

CHAPTER 5: PLANTAIN ALL OVER THE WORLD

Abubakar, Shina. "Man sentenced to a month in jail for stealing plantain." *Man sentenced to a month in jail for stealing plantain*, 20 July 2020, https://www.vanguardngr.com/2020/07/man-sentenced-to-a-month-in-jail-for-stealing-plantain/. Accessed 2020.

Eng, Monica. "Saga of a sandwich." *Chicago Tribune*, 2003, https://www.chicagotribune.com/news/ct-xpm-2003-06-18-0306180103-story.html.

FoodsFromAfrica. "5 Reasons You Should Eat More Plantain." *FoodsFromAfrica*, 30th September 2017, planted at the onset of the rainy season. This usually coincides with the planting period of several other staple crops like rice, cassava, and maize. Although plantains grow all year round, the major harvest comes between the months of November and February.

IndexBox. "Africa's Plantain Market to Reach Over 30M Tonnes by 2025." *Africa's Plantain Market to Reach Over 30M Tonnes by 2025*, 6 November 2019, https://www.globaltrademag.com/africas-plantain-market-to-reach-over-30m-tonnes-by-2025/. Accessed 2020.

ManUtdPidgin. *Twitter*, https://twitter.com/ManUtdInPidgin/status/908269210056511488.

Moser, Whet. "In Praise of the Jibarito, Chicago's Greatest Food Invention." *In Praise of the Jibarito, Chicago's Greatest Food Invention*, 15 November 2013, https://www.chicagomag.com/city-life/november-2013/in-praise-of-the-jibarito-chicagos-greatest-food-invention/. Accessed 2020.

National Museums Liverpool. "Slavery in the Caribbean." *Liverpool Museums*, https://www.liverpoolmuseums.org.uk/archaeologyofslavery/slavery-caribbean.

Precious Core. "CAMEROONIAN FOOD: BORN HOUSE PLANTI RECIPE." *CAMEROONIAN FOOD: BORN HOUSE PLANTI RECIPE*, 24 February 2016, https://www.precious-core.com/cameroonian-food-born-house-planti-recipe/#. Accessed 2020.

Rossel, Gerda. *TAXONOMIC - LINGUISTIC STUDY OF PLANTAIN IN AFRICA*, 1998. *Research School CNWS School of Asian, African and Amerindian Studies*, https://www.oecd-ilibrary.org/docserver/9789264096158-6-en.pdf?-expires=1610930432&id=id&accname=guest&check-sum=E24BFAA8651BADA32C870208D1D1DBBF.

Sula, Mike. "Origin of the Jibarito?" *Chicago Reader*, 22 July 2009, https://www.chicagoreader.com/Bleader/archives/2009/07/22/origin-of-the-jibarito.

Sweet Mother Ahayoe. https://twitter.com/sandramarilyne/status/1206664429154291712.

WorldMapper. "Plantain Production." *Plantain Production | World Mapper*, https://worldmapper.org/maps/plantain-production/. Accessed 2020.

CHAPTER 6: POLITICAL CRINKUM CRANKUM OF PLANTAIN

Adeoye, Iyabo, and Oni Omobowale. "Competitiveness and Effects of Policies on Plantain Production Systems in Southwestern Nigeria." *Introduction*, vol. Volume 6, 2014, p. 4. *Research Gate*, https://www.researchgate.net/publication/289152593_Competitiveness_and_Effects_of_Policies_on_Plantain_Production_Systems_in_Southwestern_Nigeria.

Akinfenwa, Gbenga. "How to maximize potentials of plantain." *The Guardian | Features*, 23 February 2020, https://guardian.ng/features/how-to-maximize-potentials-of-plantain/. Accessed 2020.

Balch, Oliver. "Banana pricing: the unsustainable nature of the UK's favourite fruit." *The Guardian | Sustainable Business*, 2020, https://www.theguardian.com/sustainable-business/banana-pricing-unsustainable-nature-uk.

BananaLink. "Cooperativa de Servicios Múltiples Bananera del Atlántico, R.L. (COOBANA)." *FairTrade | Coobana Panama*, https://www.fairtrade.net/news/coobana-panama. Accessed 2020.

BananaLink. "Coordinating Unions In Latin America." *BananaLink | Trade Unions Colsiba*, https://www.bananalink.org.uk/trade-unions/colsiba/. Accessed 2020.

BananaLink. "The History Of Fairtrade." *Fairtrade | What is Fairtrade | The impact of our work | The history of Fairtrade*, https://www.fairtrade.org.uk/what-is-fairtrade/the-impact-of-our-work/the-history-of-fairtrade/. Accessed 2020.

BananaLink. "Monitoring the scope and benefits of Fairtrade:

Bananas – Monitoring report, 10th Edition." *Monitoring the scope and benefits of Fairtrade: Bananas – Monitoring report, 10th Edition*, 2019, pp. 1-16. *Fairtrade | Monitoring the scope and benefits of Fairtrade: Bananas - Monitoring report: 10th edition*, https://files.fairtrade.net/publications/2019_Monitoring_Bananas_10thEd.pdf. Accessed 2020.

BananaLink. "Now I Am Bold." *Now_I_Am_Bold_800_0-2*, https://www.bananalink.org.uk/wp-content/uploads/2019/04/Now_I_Am_Bold_800_0-2.pdf.

BananaLink. "OUR WORK IN CAMEROON with Fako Agricultural Workers Union." *BananaLink | Partners | Camerooon*, https://www.bananalink.org.uk/partners/cameroon/. Accessed 2020.

BananaLink. "Our Work In Ecuador with Sinutrabe." *BananaLink | Partners Ecuador*, https://www.bananalink.org.uk/partners/ecuador/. Accessed 2020.

BananaLink. "Podcast: Veronica Brown & Simeon Green—Fairtade banana farmers from St Vincent." *Vimeo*, 2019, https://vimeo.com/343203009. Accessed 28 July 2021.

BananaLink. "Problems faced by women workers in the workplace and at home." *Women in the Banana Export Industry*, 2015, p. 10, https://www.bananalink.org.uk/wp-content/uploads/2019/04/ENG_Latin-America-report_FAO-Gender-research-2015.pdf. Accessed 2020.

BananaLink. "Women in the Banana Trade." *Banana Link | Gender Equality*, https://www.bananalink.org.uk/gender-equity/women-in-the-banana-trade/.

Barraza, Douglas, et al. "Abstract." *Pesticide use in banana and plantain production and risk perception among local actors in Talamanca, Costa Rica*, 2011. Accessed 2020.

Blittz, Matt. "The Origin of the "Slipping On A Banana Peel" Comedy Gag." *Today I Found Out, Feed Your Brain*, 29 November 2013, http://www.todayifoundout.com/index.php/2013/11/origin-slipping-banana-peel-comedy-gag/. Accessed 29 10 2020.

Chimtom, Ngala Killian. "Climate change cuts plantain production, schooling." *Scidev | Sub Suharan Africa*, 12 January 2018, https://www.scidev.net/sub-saharan-africa/news/climate-change-plantain-production-schooling/. Accessed 2020.

Coraf. "Our Organization." *Coraf | Our Organization*, https://www.coraf.org/our-organizations/. Accessed 2020.

Coraf. "Research Collaboration Stimulates Plantain Cultivation in Burkina Faso." *Research Collaboration Stimulates Plantain Cultivation in Burkina Faso*, 12 June 2019, http://www.coraf.org/2019/06/12/research-collaboration-stimulates-plantain-cultivation-in-burkina-faso/. Accessed 2020.

Daily Britain. "10th April 1633. Have a Banana." *Daily Britain*, 10 April 2018, https://dailybritain.wordpress.com/2018/04/10/10th-april-1633-have-a-banana/. Accessed 29 10 2020.

Fairtrade Foundation. "Come On In to Coobana Fairtrade Banana Plantation | Fairtrade." *YouTube*, 2018, https://www.youtube.com/watch?v=v0YXIOxmUGw. Accessed 28 July 2021.

Frazier, Maryaan. "A Short History of Pest Management." *A Short History of Pest Management*, 2010, https://extension.psu.edu/a-short-history-of-pest-management. Accessed 2020.

Fresh Plaza. "Ecuador's plantain over-supply takes a toll on prices." *Fresh Plaza*, 2020, https://www.freshplaza.com/article/9195607/ecuador-s-plantain-oversupply-takes-a-toll-on-prices/.

Fresh Plaza. "Prices of plantains skyrocket due to drought and tornadoes." *Fresh Plaza | Articles | Prices of plantains skyrocket due to drought and tornadoes*, Fresh Plaza, 11 October 2019, https://www.freshplaza.com/article/9152559/prices-of-plantains-skyrocket-due-to-drought-and-tornadoes/. Accessed 2020.

Guilford, Gwynn. "How the global banana industry is killing the world's favorite fruit." *Quartz*, 3 March 2014, https://qz.com/164029/tropical-race-4-global-banana-industry-is-killing-the-worlds-favorite-fruit/. Accessed 2020.

Hancock, James F. *Plantation Crops, Plunder and Power: Evolution and Exploitation*. Routledge, 2017.

Harford, Tim. "How refrigieration revolutionised global trade." *BBC News*, 20 November 2017, https://www.bbc.co.uk/news/business-41902071. Accessed 29 October 2020.

https://www.iita.org/news-crop/banana/. "news crop: Banana." *Banana*, https://www.iita.org/news-crop/banana/. Accessed 2020.

HUMWP.ESCEDU. "History of the Banana: 1800 to Present." *humwp.ucscedu*, https://humwp.ucsc.edu/cwh/bananas/Site/Modern%20History%20of%20the%20Banana.html. Accessed 29 10 2020.

HUMWP.UCSCEDU. "Bananas and Popular Culture." *humwp.ucscedu*, https://humwp.ucsc.edu/cwh/bananas/Site/Bananas%20and%20Popular%20Culture.html. Accessed 29 October 2020.

IndexBox. "Africa's Plantain Market to Reach Over 30M Tonnes by 2025." *Africa − Plantains − Market Analysis, Forecast, Size, Trends and Insights*, 6 November 2019, https://www.globaltrademag.com/africas-plantain-market-to-reach-over-30m-tonnes-by-2025/. Accessed 2020.

InTech Open. *Toxicology Studies - Cells, Drugs and Environment*. 2015. *InTechOpen*, https://www.intechopen.com/books/toxicology-studies-cells-drugs-and-environment/impact-of-pesticides-on-environmental-and-human-health. Accessed 2020.

International Crisis Group. "Cameroon's Anglophone Dialogue: A Work in Progress." *CrisGroup | Africa | Central Africa | Cameroon*, 26 September 2019, https://www.crisisgroup.org/africa/central-africa/cameroon/cameroons-anglophone-dialogue-work-progress. Accessed 2020.

International Institute of Tropical Agriculture. "Change of Guard: "Research is for Development."" *IITA: 50 Years After | Transforming Africa's Agriculture and Nourishing Rural Development*, pp. 29-35, https://core.ac.uk/download/pdf/132691889.pdf. Accessed 2020.

International Monetary Fund. "IMF Survey : Ghana Gets $918 Million IMF Loan to Back Growth, Jobs Plan." *IMF | Articles*, 3 April 2015, https://www.imf.org/en/News/Articles/2015/09/28/04/53/socar040315a. Accessed 2020.

kasapafmonline.com. "Mahama has collapsed Ghana; country now imports plantain from Ivory Coast – Akufo-Addo." *Modern Ghana*, 30 May 2016, https://www.modernghana.com/news/695124/mahama-has-collapsed-ghana-country-now-imports.html. Accessed 2020.

Kennedy, Alicia. "Plantains Are Cheap for Everyone But the People Who Pick Them." *Vice | Articles | Plantains Are Cheap for Everyone But the People Who Pick Them*, 22 September 2017, https://www.vice.com/en/article/gvmnpx/plantains-are-cheap-for-everyone-but-the-people-who-pick-them. Accessed 2020.

KnowledgeNuts. "The Fascinating Story of Minor Cooper Keith." *Knowledge Nuts*, 2020, https://knowledgenuts.com/2020/10/22/the-fascinating-story-of-minor-cooper-keith/.

Koeppel, Dan. *Banana: The Fate of the Fruit That Changed the World*. Hudson Street Press, 2007.

Levitt, Tom. "How Fairtrade bananas are failing migrant workers." *The Guardian | Environment*, 2020, https://www.theguardian.com/environment/2012/may/28/fair-trade-food.

Levitt, Tom. "How Fairtrade bananas are failing migrant workers." *The Guardian | Environment | Fair Trade Food*, 28 May 2012, https://www.theguardian.com/environment/2012/may/28/fair-trade-food. Accessed 2020.

McLean, Malcom D. "O. Henry in Honduras." *American Literary Realism, 1870-1910*, vol. Volume 1, no. Issue 3, 1968, pp. 39-46. *JSTOR*, https://www.jstor.org/stable/27747601?seq=1.

McPherson, Alan. *Encyclopedia of U.S Military Interventions in Latin America*. vol. 2, ABC0CLIO, 2013.

Milligan, Jessica. "'A Nasty Piece of Corporate Business' The Creation of Honduras as a Banana Republic." *https://sgs.stanford.edu/*, 2020, https://sgs.stanford.edu/research/student-research/ma-research/2016-cap-stone-research/%E2%80%9C-nasty-piece-corporate-business%E2%80%9D.

Moran, Joe. "Defining Moment: The banana returns to Britain December 30 1945." *Financial Times*, 1 August 2009, https://www.ft.com/content/c275b5b2-7a73-11de-8c34-00144fe-abdc0. Accessed 29 10 2020.

NPR. "America's Gone Bananas: Here's How It Happened." *America's Gone Bananas: Here's How It Happened*, 2020, https://www.npr.org/2012/06/02/154153252/americas-gone-ba-nanas-heres-how-it-happened?t=1624653000530.

NYU Langone Health. "Genetically Modified Organisms: The "Golden Rice" Debate." *HomeGenetically Modified Organisms: The "Golden Rice" Debate*, https://med.nyu.edu/highschoolbio-ethics/genetically-modified-organisms-%E2%80%9Cgold-en-rice%E2%80%9D-debate. Accessed 2020.

Ordnance Survey. "How the Great Famine Changed the Landscape of Ireland." *Osi. Ie | Blog*, 8 June 2018, https://www.osi.ie/blog/

how-the-great-famine-changed-the-landscape-of-ireland/. Accessed 2020.

Pesticide Action Network UK. "Impacts of pesticides on our health." *Health Effects of Pesticides*, https://www.pan-uk.org/health-effects-of-pesticides/. Accessed 2020.

"Planting for Food & Jobs." *Mofa.Gov*, https://mofa.gov.gh/site/programmes/pfj.

"Podcast: Veronica Brown & Simeon Green - Fairtade banana farmers from St Vincent." *Vimeo*, Vimeo, 2019, https://vimeo.com/343203009. Accessed 28 July 2021.

Powderly, William G. "How Infection Shaped History: Lessons From The Irish Famine." *Trans Am Clin Climatol Assocation*, 2019, pp. 127–135. *PubMed Central*, https://www.ncbi.nlm.nih.gov/pmc/articles/PMC6735970/. Accessed 2020.

ProMusa. "FHIA-01." *ProMusa*, https://www.promusa.org/FHIA-01. Accessed 2020.

ProMusa. "Tropical Race 4." *Tropical race 4 - TR4 | Improving the understanding*, https://www.promusa.org/Tropical+race+4+-+TR4. Accessed 2020.

Queensland Government. "Panama disease tropical race 4 (TR4)." *Panama TR4 frequently asked questions*, 2020, https://www.business.qld.gov.au/industries/farms-fishing-forestry/agriculture/crop-growing/priority-pest-disease/panama-disease. Accessed 2020.

@ronkelawal   https://twitter.com/ronkelawal/
status/1136330334658879488.

Science Daily. "Study uncovers cause of pesticide exposure,
Parkinson's link." *ScienceDaily*, 2018, https://www.sciencedaily.
com/releases/2018/05/180523133158.htm. Accessed 2020.

Stromberg, Joseph. "The improbable rise of the banana,
America's most popular fruit." *Vox*, 27 October 2020, https://
www.vox.com/2016/3/29/11320900/banana-rise.

Sylla, Ndongo Samba. "Fairtrade is an unjust movement that
serves the rich." *The Guardian | Global Development | Fairtrade
Unjust Movement Serves Rich*, 11 September 2014, https://www.
theguardian.com/global-development/2014/sep/05/fair-
trade-unjust-movement-serves-rich. Accessed 2020.

Sylla, Ndongo Samba. "Fairtrade only really benefits super-
markets. A rethink is needed." *The Guardian | Comment Is Free |
Fairtrade-benefits-supermarkets-global-south-outdated-model*, 4 August
2017, https://www.theguardian.com/commentisfree/2017/
aug/04/fairtrade-benefits-supermarkets-global-south-outdat-
ed-model. Accessed 2020.

Tenkouano, Abdou, et al. "Promising High-Yielding
Tetraploid Plantain-Bred Hybrids in West Africa." *Hindawi |
Journals*, 21 April 2019, https://www.hindawi.com/journals/
ija/2019/3873198/. Accessed 2020.

Thompson, Stuart. "The quest to save the banana from extinction." *theconversation*, 18 April 2019, https://theconversation.
com/the-quest-to-save-the-banana-from-extinction-112256.
Accessed 2020.

Trend Economy. "Annual International Trade Statistics by Country (HS02)." *Annual International Trade Statistics by Country (HS02)*, 2021, https://trendeconomy.com/data/h2/Ghana/0803. Accessed 2021.

University of Exeter. "Impact of climate change on global banana yields revealed." *Impact of climate change on global banana yields revealed*, 2 September 2019, https://www.exeter.ac.uk/news/research/title_732684_en.html. Accessed 2020.

ENDNOTES

CHAPTER 2

1   *The History and Domestication of Bananas*, 2018
2   (De Langhe 6)
3   (Palmer 1932, 262
4   (De Langhe 1996, 6)
5   Carney, 2011, 114)
6   (The Cambridge History of Africa 1978, 314)
7   (Carney, 2011, 41-42)
8   (HUMWP.UCSC.EDU, n.d.)
9   (Rossel, 1998, 4)
10 (ProMusa, n.d.)
11 (Mindzie et al., 2001, abstract)
12 (Carney, 2011, 40)
13 (Carney, 2011, 40)
14 (Carney, 2011, 40)
15 (Carney, 2011, 40)
16 (Carney, 2011, 114)
17 (Rossel, 1998, 19)
18 (Rossel, 1998, 19)
19 (Blench, 2009, 367)
20 (Kpone-Tonwe, 1987, 110)
21 (Kpone-Tonwe, 1987, 110)
22 (WorldMapper, 2018)
23 (Fresh Plaza, 2020)
24 (Marin et al., 1998, 969)
25 (Marin et al., 1998, 969)
26 (Marin et al., 1998, 968)
27 (Marin et al., 1998, 968)
28 (Marin et al., 1998, 968)
29 (Marin et al., 1998, 968)

30	(Diaz del Castillo, 2012)
31	(Luscombe, n.d.)
32	(The National Archives, n.d.)
33	(National Archives, n.d.)
34	(University of Glasgow, n.d.)
35	(National Museums Liverpool, n.d.)
36	(McFadden, 2019)
37	(Velez, 2017, 26)
38	(Barkham, 1999)
39	(Gibbings, n.d.)
40	(European Council of the European Union, n.d.)
41	(Carney, 2011, 54)
42	(Carney, 2011, 114)
43	(Siegler & O'Neill, 2019)
1	(Macbryde, 2009, 16)

CHAPTER 5

1	(WorldMapper)
2	(IndexBox)
3	(FoodsFromAfrica)
4	(Abubakar)
5	(Precious Core)
6	(Moser)

CHAPTER 6

1	(StromXberg)
2	(Stromberg)
3	(Blittz)
4	(Koeppel 67)
5	(Koeppel 68)
6	(HUMWP.UCSCEDU)

7	(Harford)
8	(Daily Britain)
9	(McLean #)
10	(KnowledgeNuts)
11	(Koeppel 59, 60)
12	(Koeppel 60)
13	(Hancock 37)
14	(Koeppel 60)
15	(Koeppel 64)
16	(Koeppel 64)
17	(Milligan)
18	(Koeppel 69)
19	(Koeppel 88)
20	(Balch)
21	(Balch)
22	(NPR)
23	(BananaLink)
24	(BananaLink)
25	(Akinfenwa)
26	(Adeoye and Omobowale 4)
27	(Akinfenwa)
28	(Akinfenwa)
29	(International Monetary Fund)
30	(kasapafmonline.com)
31	(Trend Economy)
32	("Planting for Food & Jobs")
33	(Trend Economy)
34	(Frazier)
35	(Barraza et al.)
36	(Barraza et al.)
37	(InTech Open 1)
38	(Pesticide Action Network UK)
39	(InTech Open 1)

40	(InTech Open)
41	(Science Daily)
42	(BananaLink 10)
43	(BananaLink 12)
44	(Queensland Government)
45	(Thompson)
46	(Powderly)
47	(Ordnance Survey)
48	(Guilford)
49	(ProMusa)
50	(ProMusa)
51	(Guilford)
52	(Guilford)
53	(Guilford)
54	(IndexBox)
55	(NYU Langone Health)
56	(ProMusa)
57	(https://www.iita.org/news-crop/banana/)
58	(Coraf)
59	(Coraf)
60	(Tenkouano et al.)
61	(International Institute of Tropical Agriculture 35)
62	(BananaLink)
63	(BananaLink)
64	(BananaLink)
65	(BananaLink)
66	(BananaLink)
67	(Fairtrade Foundation)
68	(BananaLink 1-16)
69	(Kennedy)
70	(Levitt)
71	(Sylla)
72	(Sylla)

73   (@ronkelawal)
74   (Fresh Plaza)
75   (University of Exeter)
76   (Chimtom)
77   (Chimtom)

ACKNOWLEDGEMENTS

I can't, without omission, mention everyone that has contributed to the writing of this book. From the coffee shop staff who let me stay that extra 15 minutes after closing, to my friends who haven't stopped asking me for pre-order dates when all I want to do is crawl into a hole. But first and foremost, I would like to thank, with absolute sincerity, the Black British diaspora. Of newer generations and old. The people who have helped me navigate this land with an unshakable belief in who I am, where I'm from and the cultures I represent. Without you all, this book and all the events leading up to it would not have been possible. Gang.

To my Godson PJ, whose continuous growth has inspired me to do the same. You are not yet at the stage in life where you'll be able to read this. Still, I feel compelled to write to you anyway.

You've changed all our lives for the better and for what it's worth, you are proof that Plantain is for all ages. Seeing you smile is an invaluable joy. I love you, mate. Please don't grow up to be a disappointment. I can no longer take these words back.

To my friend, my sister from another and my editor. Mags, Magzz, Magdelegne. Magdalene Abraha. Who would have thought we'd end up like this? In our first year in college, we were opps and we didn't think highly of each other. Fast forward to 2021 and you have given me more than I could ask for in a friend and an editor. Thank you for thinking of me as a writer and giving life to an idea I would have never thought possible. You have brought out what I hope is the best in me and have made this process easier, even at times when I questioned myself. Your levels of patience, understanding and tact are a blessing and I hope you walk into all the good things you deserve.

And finally, to my family. Mum, Richard and Ellen. I love you all more than words can describe. Nothing happens without you.

ABOUT THE AUTHOR

Rui da Silva is a producer, creative practitioner and youth worker focusing on the social mobility of young, working-class people. Rui has collaborated with Caleb Femi, Zia Ahmed, Lex Amor, Lionheartfelt, Latir Thakur, Sophia Thakur, Bush Theatre, Westway Trust, Khidr Collective, Young Hackney, The Barbican, The Tate Modern, Artsadmin and The Showroom.

Rui is also the founder *AfroEats*, a magazine that celebrates Afro-Caribbean home-cooks in London. His campaign to crowdsource funds for his mother's university tuition was featured in *Vice*, *BuzzFeed* and BBC Two's *Victoria Derbyshire* show.